Collaboration Begins With You

Be A Silo Buster

Ken Blanchard
Jane Ripley
Eunice Parisi-Carew

EasyRead Large

Copyright Page from the Original Book

Collaboration Begins with You

Berrett-Koehler Publishers, Inc.
1333 Broadway, Suite 1000
Oakland, CA 94612-1921
Tel: (510) 817-2277, Fax: (510) 817-2278
www.bkconnection.com

Ordering information for print editions

Quantity sales. Special discounts are available on quantity purchases by corporations, associations, and others. For details, contact the "Special Sales Department" at the Berrett-Koehler address above.

Individual sales. Berrett-Koehler publications are available through most bookstores. They can also be ordered directly from Berrett-Koehler: Tel: (800) 929-2929; Fax: (802) 864-7626; www.bkconnection.com

Orders for college textbook/course adoption use. Please contact Berrett-Koehler: Tel: (800) 929-2929; Fax: (802) 864-7626.

Orders by U.S. trade bookstores and wholesalers. Please contact Ingram Publisher Services, Tel: (800) 509-4887; Fax: (800) 838-1149; E-mail: customer.service@ingrampublisherservices.com; or visit www.ingram publisherservices.com/Ordering for details about electronic ordering.

Berrett-Koehler and the BK logo are registered trademarks of Berrett-Koehler Publishers, Inc.

First Edition

Hardcover print edition ISBN 978-1-62656-617-0
PDF e-book ISBN 978-1-62656-618-7
IDPF e-book ISBN 978-1-62656-619-4

2015-1

Production Management: Michael Bass Associates

Cover Design: Irene Morris Design

TABLE OF CONTENTS

Ken Blanchard

To my father and mother, Ted and Dorothy Blanchard, who came from completely different backgrounds but modeled collaboration in over fifty years of marriage.

Jane Ripley

To my late father, Bill (William) Anderson, who always taught me it is better to collaborate than to just cooperate. To my mother, Betty, who provided the support for my research and the confidence to write it up as a story. You are my inspiration.

Eunice Parisi-Carew

I would like to dedicate this book not to a person, but to a community of people who make up the faculty of NTL Institute. NTL is an organization committed to democratizing organizations and social justice. These values are deeply instilled in its members, and it continues to be a guiding force in my life.

PART I

A Journey to Collaboration

CHAPTER 1

A Troubling Conversation

"It was the worst shareholder meeting I've endured in years. The worst! Everybody could see the numbers plain and clear: the Primo project produced no profit. No profit! Zero. Zip. None!" Jim Camilleri, CEO of Cobalt, Inc., punctuated the point by slamming his fist on his desk.

Dave Oakman, the division head in charge of the Primo project, had never seen his boss this angry before. It was making him nervous. He kept his mouth shut to give Jim time to blow off more steam.

"The whole point of this project was to put some distance between Cobalt and our competition. The idea, in case you missed it, was to generate some revenue for capital investments and to reward shareholders. The fundamentals were great. There was absolutely no reason we couldn't have made money on this thing—other than lousy project management." Jim leaned forward and looked Dave in the eye. "Can you give me a better reason? What happened here?"

"It's a long story, Jim."

"Let's hear it."

"We had departments operating in silos. A lot of people were trying to protect their own interests rather than make the project a success."

"Why don't you break that down for me, Dave. What are you talking about?" Jim's mouth was a straight, grim line.

Dave hesitated. Should he tell the truth, or should he bend it? He knew exactly what the problem was. What he didn't know was whether it was safe to divulge. Considering Jim's current mood, telling the whole truth could get him fired.

Dave decided he should fudge it, or at least try to. It was what he usually did—and it usually worked.

"Primo had some great moments." Dave began with an air of confidence—but he knew he was flying by the seat of his pants.

"Great moments? Not from where I'm sitting," Jim said.

"As you said, the fundamentals of the Primo project were solid. We just encountered some hiccups."

"Bleeding money is not a case of hiccups. Quit trivializing this! I want some straight answers." Jim's eyes were steely.

Dave recognized that fudging was not going to work this time. He had to come clean.

"The truth is, Jim, the group didn't really work as a cohesive unit. Rival departments undermined the project. As long as they got their job done on schedule and their department made a profit, they didn't care what happened to Primo." A bead of sweat on Dave's forehead betrayed his uneasiness.

"Can you be specific?" Jim asked.

"For example, I asked for a few of our newer associates to join the project. They had great energy and ideas, but they kept getting sidelined by the department heads who wanted all the glory. Some of our best people were kept off this project by their own leaders." Dave could hear the desperation in his own voice.

"Any leaders in particular?" Jim asked.

Dave thought about Wayne Lundgren, the veteran manager of the research and development department. Just last week Dave had witnessed Wayne brushing off a helpful suggestion made by Sarah McKenzie, a young engineer in his department.

"I'd rather not name names," Dave said at last. "Besides, it's not the people who are the problem. It's the whole culture around here." The words were out of his mouth before he had weighed them. Now he wondered if he'd said too much.

"Names don't matter, anyway," said Jim impatiently. "*You* were in charge of Primo. *You* should have fixed it!"

"It's not that simple, Jim. Certain department heads around here have a lot of power, and they don't hesitate to use it to their advantage. You know Cobalt is riddled with politics."

Jim shook his head. "Politics is a way of life. It's part of the environment we live in. I expect my top managers to know how to navigate through the obstacles. And that includes *you.*"

He's not getting it, thought Dave. Doing his best to keep the defensiveness out of his voice, he said, "Jim, I'm telling you about a problem that's beyond my scope to manage. This is about Cobalt. The company is made up of all kinds of self-serving silos. We offer no incentives that encourage people to work together toward organizational goals. Managers get promotions and bonuses based on their own individual success and the success of their siloed groups—regardless of the success of the projects they work on or the company as a whole."

There, he'd said it. He caught his breath, feeling relief and fear at the same time.

Jim got up from his desk and began to pace. "I need time to think about what you're saying here. In the meantime, remember that as the division vice president, you're expected to fix these issues you're complaining about. You should be coming to me with solutions, not problems." He shook his head. "How many times do I have to—" He left the sentence unfinished.

Dave held his breath. *Is Jim going to fire me?*

A long silence followed. Finally, Jim walked to the door and opened it, making it clear the meeting was over.

As Dave walked out, Jim said quietly, "I want a full report about what went wrong with Primo, along with your recommendations, on my desk in two weeks." He paused. "I'll just leave it at that. I need to do some thinking, too."

CHAPTER 2

A Well Timed Visitor

Back in his office, Dave stared at his computer screen. A calendar reminder popped up with a *ding.* His eyes locked on the little window but the information didn't register. His mind was replaying his meeting with Jim—particularly Jim's last words: *I want a full report on my desk in two weeks.... I need to do some thinking, too.* Dave wondered if his job was on the line. Was firing Dave what Jim needed to think about? He was demanding, but he usually didn't make threats.

Ding. The reminder popped up again, urging Dave to take notice. When the information finally sank in, he grabbed his phone, stuffed his laptop into his briefcase, and hurried out of the building. Saying "Call home" to his phone as he ran through the parking lot, Dave then cursed under his breath. *Damn, I'm late again.*

Dee picked up on the fourth ring. "Hello?"

"Honey, I'm just now leaving the office. I'm sorry, but I'm going to be late."

Dee sighed. "I'm pouring wine now. We'll save a glass for you."

Twenty minutes later, Dave pulled into the driveway. He walked around the side of the house and entered through the back door. He slipped into the bathroom, cleaned up, took a deep breath, and prepared to greet his sister-in-law from the UK. This would be the first time he'd seen her in several years.

She spied him as soon as he entered the living room. "Hello, Dave! How are you?"

The years had been kind to Beattie Anderson. Dave thought she looked like a wiser, more dignified version of the blonde, twenty-something maid of honor at his wedding. She stood eye to eye with him, offering a handshake and a warm smile. He leaned in for a quick embrace.

"Great to see you, Beattie. I'm doing well, thanks." *Was he?* Now that he thought about it, Dave felt stressed out. He gestured to the glass in her hand. "I see you have some wine. Don't mind if I do." He poured some wine from a decanter into a glass and promptly took a drink.

Dee came in from the kitchen. "Dinner is served."

Beattie and Dave made their way to the dining room, where the table had been set for three with the good china and silver.

"Wow," said Dave as they took their seats. "This is quite a spread."

"Of course it is," Dee replied. "It's not every day I get to cook for my sister."

Dee tapped her fork against her wine glass and a clear note rang out. "Before we start our appetizers—or as they say across the pond, *starters*—I'd like to make a toast." Dee turned to their guest. "To my dear sister, Beattie, and her recent success!"

"Hear, hear," said Dave, smiling and raising his glass.

"I couldn't think of a better way to celebrate the sale of my company than to get over to the States for a good visit," said Beattie. They all clinked glasses and began to eat.

"So, Beattie, I hear you made a killing on the London Stock Exchange," said Dave.

"Yes, yes, I did," Beattie admitted. "Now I have the time and the money to come and see you in sunny San Diego. You have no idea how much I could do with some sunshine right now."

"So it's raining in London?"

"God, yes. It's been the wettest April since records began—and that's saying a *lot,*" Beattie said with a laugh.

Still reeling from his meeting with Jim, Dave found it difficult to engage in polite conversation. After all, there was only so much they could discuss about the sun in San Diego and the rain in London.

Beattie took the initiative. "Dave, what's happening at work these days? Dee told me you recently headed up a big project—*Primo* was the name, I believe?"

"Yes, Primo. I found out today that it was a failure—and it looks like I'll take the hit." *Did I really just say that in front of Dee's sister?*

Dave thought. He was immediately embarrassed at his lack of discretion in the presence of such a successful woman.

"Oh, Dave," said Dee, "that's awful."

Beattie was sympathetic. "Gosh, I'm so sorry. If you don't mind me asking, what do you think the problem was?"

"Problems *plural*," he corrected. "It was one of those projects where if something could go wrong, it went wrong."

"Sod's Law!"

"Excuse me?"

"Oh, nothing—it's a British saying for things that go wrong."

"Ah—here we call it Murphy's Law," said Dave with a nod. "Anyway, I had three departments working on this project, and each of the department managers wanted to lead the whole thing. When the managers weren't fighting, the team members started acting out, claiming they needed to take care of their bosses' interests."

Having heard Dave's stories about Primo as the project had evolved, and being an experienced HR executive herself, Dee joined in. "That's what silos are all about—everyone protecting their own interests. Talk about egos!"

Beattie nodded thoughtfully. "Sounds tough. I had similar issues at Blenheim when we really started to grow—self-serving managers and siloed departments. I hadn't realized that moving from a startup to a midsized company would cause so many growing pains. My executive team and I had to really think about the most efficient method of operation—something that would ensure excellent results *and* human satisfaction. In the end, we realized we would never achieve our goals without genuine collaboration."

"What kind of collaboration? What do you mean?" Dave asked.

"I mean we had to focus on everything from our vision and values to how individuals at every level could feel they were making a real contribution. It was a huge culture change for everyone. Managers had to give up their silos and their perceptions of power and start focusing on the collective good rather than on their own gain."

Dave let out a laugh. "Ha! There's an impossible dream—getting department heads to give up their fiefdoms. How on earth did you manage *that?*"

"Dave, please," said Dee quietly.

"It's all right," said Beattie. She smiled at Dave. "I don't blame you for scoffing—it took quite a bit of time for us all to become what we called 'silo busters' and to make the shift to a collaborative culture. But we did it—with fantastic results. I'd be happy to chat it through with you if you think it would help."

"Silo busters, huh?" said Dave, unconvinced. "Thanks—I'll think about it."

CHAPTER 3

A Sensible Start

That night Dave hardly slept a wink. His restlessness kept Dee awake, too. She finally gave up trying to sleep and switched on the bedside lamp.

"What is it, honey?" she asked.

Dave sighed heavily. "It's the Primo project. The end product wasn't bad—but it was a financial bomb for the company."

"Yes, you mentioned that. How bad of a bomb are you talking about?"

"A *zero profit* bomb."

A long silence followed. From Dee's experience, she understood there might be implications for her husband.

"Do you think you're going to survive this?"

"I don't know. In a couple of weeks I have to give Jim a full report about what went wrong and how to keep it from happening again. It's not going to be easy. I know Beattie said she would give me a few pointers, but it's going to take more than a pep talk for me to figure out how to get through to the department managers. I'm dealing with some very arrogant personalities."

"You know, Dave," said Dee thoughtfully, "sometimes the best way to get other people to give up their egos is for you to give up yours first."

Taken aback, Dave propped himself up on his elbows and glared at his wife. "What the heck is *that* supposed to mean?

"What it means is that maybe, in the grand scheme of things, there's a reason Beattie just happens to be visiting us right now. She's been where you are and has come through it with great success. Why don't you get your ego out of the way and ask her for some help?" Dee switched off the light and turned away from Dave.

Frowning, Dave lay down again. Dee was his biggest cheerleader when things were going well. But he could also count on her to challenge him—and to be brutally honest, if necessary, when she had a point to make.

Dave suddenly tossed off the blanket and got out of bed.

"Dave, it's four in the morning! Get back here!" Dee called in a loud whisper.

"Nah—I'm just keeping you up." He put on his robe, closed the bedroom door, and headed downstairs. He figured he might as well have a snack as long as he was wide awake.

As Dave approached the kitchen, he swore he could smell toast. He soon realized he wasn't the only insomniac in the house.

"Hi. I couldn't sleep—it's that awful eight-hour time difference," Beattie said, shaking her head. "I hope you don't mind, but I helped myself to tea and toast. I see my dear sister thoughtfully bought English toasting bread." She laughed. "I don't know why they call it that. It's nothing like our toast."

Dave poured himself a glass of milk and put a piece of bread in the toaster. "And your chips are nothing like ours!" He sat down wearily. "I couldn't sleep, either."

"Is the Primo project keeping you awake?"

"Yeah." Dave took a deep breath. "Beattie, I'd like to take you up on your offer to help me figure out how to get all of our people to work together. Maybe what helped your company succeed can help our company, too."

"Brilliant!" exclaimed Beattie, toasting Dave with her tea cup.

"I think we'd better get started right away if I'm going to try to singlehandedly change our entire company culture," said Dave, only half joking.

Not missing a beat, Beattie began. "All right, then. Well, as I mentioned at dinner, collaboration is the key to a high performing organization."

Dave shook his head. "I've been thinking about that since you mentioned it—but we already have teams. In fact, we're pretty smooth when it comes to running individual teams."

"Dave, collaboration is a whole order of magnitude beyond teams. It's in the DNA of the company culture. It's the mindset of every member of the organization—the air the company breathes. It's an environment that promotes communication, learning, maximum contribution, and innovation—which, of course, all lead to healthy profits."

"Hold on a minute," said Dave. He went into his study and returned with a notepad and pen. He began to write as Beattie spoke.

"First, let me give you our guiding principle of collaboration: *Collaboration begins with YOU.*"

"You sound just like my boss," said Dave as he wrote. "No matter what reasons I gave him about why Primo failed, he said, 'I don't care about any of that. *You* were in charge and it was *your* job to make it work.'"

"In one sense, he's a wise man," said Beattie, "but in another sense, he isn't—because he put all of the accountability in your court. He never acknowledged *his* duty as CEO to create a collaborative culture throughout the organization. When we say 'Collaboration begins with you,' we're talking about *every person in the company* taking responsibility, from the CEO to the people at entry level. Let me see if I can explain this better. Give me the pen."

On Dave's pad, Beattie wrote:

Heart → Head → Hands

"I'm going to teach you a simple way to understand how a collaborative culture works. Each word—Heart, Head, and Hands—represents a different domain of collaboration."

"I've heard of that model before, but isn't it Head first, and then Heart and Hands?"

"Not in this case. At Blenheim, we refer to collaboration as an *inside-out mindset.* It has to start on the inside, with the Heart. If you don't get the Heart part right, you'll never be effective as a collaborative leader, because the Heart is really *who you are* as a collaborator—your character and intentions. Then it moves to the Head, which is about *what you know*—your beliefs and attitudes about collaboration. And finally, the Hands are all about *what you do*—your actions and behavior during collaboration."

Pen in hand again and writing quickly, Dave said, "This is interesting, Beattie, but I owe Jim a do-or-die report in two weeks. Where do I start?"

"Why don't we start with the Heart domain and see where that takes you today?"

Dave nodded his head in agreement.

"The focus here is for you to answer this question: As a leader at Cobalt, do you think all the brains are in your office, or are there bright people around you? If you think you're the one with all the answers, I guarantee collaboration won't occur if you are involved."

Beattie's statement caught Dave off guard. *First there was Dee's remark about my ego, and now this! I'd been thinking Wayne and the other managers were the major obstacle to our progress with Primo, and now Beattie is implying that I'm part of the problem!*

"When your heart is right," continued Beattie, "you want to bring out the best in others. Tap into the wealth of knowledge all around you. Utilize different opinions and perspectives. A few people at my company came up with a phrase that beautifully captures the essence of this concept: 'None of us is as smart as all of us.' As a leader, it's your job to get everyone to share what they know. Let people bring their brains to work! And this is important: the more diverse the perspectives in the room, the better."

"But if you put a lot of people together with different opinions on how things should be done, won't they all end up arguing?" Dave asked.

Beattie took the last bite of her toast and said, "Maybe. But when everyone has a collaborative mindset, conflict can be constructive. There's an old saying: 'If two people always agree, one of them is unnecessary.'"

Dave smiled. "Yeah, I know that saying. But it seems to me that conflict would be the opposite of collaboration."

"Not at all—conflict can be very healthy within a collaborative group, as long as everyone sticks to the issues and things don't get personal. It can lead to breakthrough learnings and innovation."

Beattie yawned. "At last, I feel tired. Time for a nap, I think. Can we continue this later?"

"Sure—and thanks," said Dave as he scribbled *Utilize differences* on his pad. *If conflict is healthy, Cobalt managers are Olympic athletes,* he thought. He'd have to ask Beattie to explain that concept in more detail.

***

When he reached his office at Cobalt, Dave opened his briefcase, took out his notepad, and studied his notes. When he got to the phrase *Collaboration begins with you,* the word *YOU* screamed out at him as if it were saying, *"YOU, Dave! YOU have to fix this!"*

Dave frowned. He had two pressing concerns: Would Jim agree to give him time to sort all this out and fix the problems they'd discussed? And would Beattie be able to teach him everything he needed to know before she went home to London?

He started thinking about the Heart domain and the phrase *None of us is as smart as all of us.* He had to admit it made sense. Just then there was a knock on his office door.

"Come in," Dave called.

"Hey, Dave," said the young woman as she hurried in and placed a folder on Dave's desk. "I emailed you my notes on Primo that you asked for, but I thought you might want to see the rest of my file." She paused and glanced at his face. "No offense, but you look beat. Everything okay?"

Dave motioned for her to sit down. He liked Sarah McKenzie. One of the newer engineers in Wayne's department, she'd graduated near the top of her class at Berkeley. Dave could see her leading some major projects at Cobalt in the future if she could get out from under Wayne's thumb. But as he had shared with Jim, senior managers didn't seem to care much about potential contributions that could be made by younger staff. New hires did receive a good orientation to the field, however, which made them attractive to the competition. As a result, bright young employees didn't stay long—their average tenure was about eighteen months.

"Let's just say I had a tough meeting last night," Dave replied.

Sarah looked concerned. "Sorry to hear that. Anything I can do to help?"

"Actually, yes—I'd like to pick your brain for a few minutes, if you have time."

"Sure!"

"My very successful sister-in-law suggested to me that to get rid of the silos around here, we need to create a collaborative environment at Cobalt." Dave handed Sarah his notepad.

"Hmmm," Sarah spoke as she read. "'*None of us is as smart as all of us.*' Sounds like an interesting concept, but I don't know—it might be a hard sell."

"She said in order for collaboration to work, every person at every level has to take responsibility; in other words, collaboration begins with you. It starts with the Heart—who you are. It's about your character and your intentions. Managers need to be open to hearing ideas from their people. And I think people want to contribute—to bring their brains to work. We have a lot of diverse people with loads of experience we could be tapping into. What do you think?"

"We do have all different kinds of people working here," said Sarah, "but a lot of them don't get much of a chance to 'bring their brains to work,' as you just said. I've seen younger workers get shut down when they tried to share their thoughts. People don't feel empowered to express themselves. Bosses seem to want to keep them in their place, doing nothing beyond their current role and function. I think this is an issue for a lot of new people here."

"Has that been your experience as well?" Dave asked, knowing what her answer would be.

Sarah shrugged. "Pretty much. I've learned a lot here. I'd really love to contribute more, but Wayne seldom asks my opinion on anything. I get the impression it's because I haven't been out of college long. But I've been learning and studying for *six years*—I've done lots of research and I've learned from the very best professors. I really want to be part of the success of this company. But when I don't get to use what I know and what I've learned, it feels like it doesn't have any meaning—like I'm wasting my time."

"What do you see as a possible solution? Or do you think there is one?" asked Dave, digging for more feedback.

Sarah paused. "To be honest with you, what you just said about each person taking responsibility is making me think. *I'm* really the one who's responsible for ensuring my opinion is heard. If collaboration begins with me, it's up to *me* to make my intention clear that I want to contribute more."

"You're right. We can't always rely on managers to solicit everyone's opinions—people like you need to take the initiative and speak up. You can be a silo buster! In fact, you're doing it right now."

"What do you mean?"

"You're not in my department, but here we are, brainstorming ways to make the whole company better. If that's not silo busting, I don't know what is."

"You know, with the rich diversity in our company, if everyone started to really talk *and* listen to each other like we're doing, it could be a powerful thing," said Sarah.

"When you say *diversity,* what does it mean to you?"

"Well, it goes without saying that diverse cultural backgrounds bring very important perspectives to the table. We should also think beyond things like nationality, age, and gender. For example, military veterans have unique and valuable points of view, shaped by their service. And take extroverts and introverts—we can't just assume extroverts have better ideas because they are more outgoing. Some people may need a little encouragement to speak their mind. Also, it's not necessarily true that higher educational levels alone bring innovation—someone with a BA who has traveled the world will have different knowledge to share than someone with a PhD who has never left California. But we won't hear these perspectives if we aren't open to utilizing these differences."

"Wow. You're giving me a lot to think about," said Dave.

"Ditto," Sarah said, smiling. "Isn't that what silo busters do?"

Dave couldn't help but notice how energetic Sarah became when she realized he cared about her opinion. This kind of interaction didn't happen often at Cobalt.

Sarah stood up. "If newer people in the company, like me, believed that our managers valued our opinions and wanted to hear them the way you did just now, I know we'd be more engaged—and we'd keep contributing. Because you know what, Dave?" She smiled and handed him back his note pad. "*None* of us is as smart as *all* of us."

CHAPTER 4

Utilize Differences

Dave hurried home, eager to have another chat with Beattie. He was aware that time was ticking by and he needed to start writing his report for Jim. The house was empty when he arrived. Walking through the kitchen, he noticed a note on the counter in Dee's handwriting. It read simply, "Gone to the beach."

I'm glad they're taking advantage of the weather, thought Dave.

***

Dave was barbecuing lamb kebabs and Italian vegetables for dinner when Dee and Beattie returned. After they'd enjoyed their meal and the dishes had been cleared, Dave sat down with his notepad and pen, cleared his throat, and gave Beattie a hopeful look.

"Dave!" Dee chided. "I'm happy that you're reaching out to Beattie, but let the woman digest her dinner."

"Sorry," he said.

Beattie jumped in. "No, Dee, this is fine. Dave has a short time frame to figure things out. Besides, I'm enjoying it."

Dee walked over and put her hands on Dave's shoulders. "All right. Would you mind using your office? I'd like a little quiet time to do some writing."

"Of course," he said.

Beattie admired the décor as they entered Dave's comfortably appointed study. She took one of the chairs across the coffee table from Dave.

"I was talking with a coworker named Sarah McKenzie today about how collaboration has to start from the Heart, and when you have a heart for collaboration, you utilize the diverse opinions of the people around you. Sarah pointed out that it's hard for managers to consider different perspectives if they never ask people what they think."

"Tell me about Sarah," said Beattie.

"She's one of our young engineers. I think she shows tremendous promise. As far as I'm concerned, she's just the sort of talent we should be grooming to take over a senior role in the company someday. When I explained the concept that collaboration starts with you, she even started thinking about what she could do differently to make her voice heard. Once that happened, our whole conversation changed. She wasn't afraid to speak truthfully."

"That's marvelous, Dave. In many organizations, people are prevented from offering suggestions or even enjoying their work because of leaders who don't realize the advantages of asking for feedback—as you did with Sarah."

Dave nodded. "Yes, Sarah's seen that behavior in action more than once at Cobalt. In fact, she had several ideas on the Primo project that were ignored by some senior leaders because she wasn't part of their team—and even by her own leader because she's, you know, *young.* I found out she really wants to contribute, and when it doesn't happen, she gets pretty frustrated."

"We had the same problem at Blenheim," said Beattie. "The older generation wouldn't listen to the younger generation because the young people had no experience, let alone tenure with the company. Some managers didn't want people in their department to get selected for tasks beyond their current responsibilities, and so on. It sounds like both you and Sarah know how that goes."

Dave smiled. It was as if Beattie knew exactly what the Primo project had been like.

"So, Dave," said Beattie, "let's talk about this. The key is to continuously promote a collaborative mindset and culture within the company."

"Right. The air we breathe."

"To do that at Blenheim, we decided we wouldn't promote any manager unless they clearly demonstrated that they had worked collaboratively. That means they had to have worked with and shared their talent with other departments on at least one project. Plus, their colleagues had to confirm they had contributed willingly. And it wasn't just about their contribution—they needed to show they were willing to ask for and consider the opinions of others, and even utilize an idea they might not agree with if it was for the greater good."

"Accepting ideas you don't agree with—that's remarkable," said Dave. "So what I'm hearing is that if a company really wants people to collaborate, it has to be part of the reward system. No collaboration, no promotion. Does that philosophy have to start with the top management?"

"Absolutely!" Beattie insisted. "I've never heard of a bottom-up reward and punishment system, have you?" She continued with a smile. "Because collaboration begins with each individual, the only people who should be promoted to leadership positions are those who allow others to contribute. By considering ideas from everyone, you will not only deepen the collective mindset of collaboration within the company, but also drive out silos and increase productivity."

"So it sounds like the natural result of utilizing different perspectives is that people are more engaged because they feel their opinions are important. And you get the benefit of a ton of ideas and solutions to problems."

"Exactly. Innovation rarely comes from just one group. It's still hard, though, for people to take a risk and put an idea forward for fear that it will be dismissed without consideration. To counter that fear, at Blenheim we have brainstorming sessions where we encourage suggestions from everyone at every level. At these sessions, staff members mix with experts, peers, supervisors, and executives. It's a great learning opportunity that increases engagement with the company all around."

"Wow, lots of wins there," said Dave.

As Beattie talked, it became obvious to Dave why she was so successful in business. Her enthusiasm was infectious.

"I've been at some great sessions," Beattie said. "My newest recruits told me how exciting it was to have their ideas heard by revered experts and senior leaders. For some it was the first time they had ever felt trusted or empowered to speak their mind. I've seen employee work passion go through the roof during those meetings."

They both sat thoughtfully for a moment.

"Something you mentioned earlier still baffles me," said Dave. "It was about conflict actually being healthy."

"Seems like an oxymoron, doesn't it?"

"At this point, yes. In my report for Jim on what went wrong with Primo, I need to include recommendations on how to ensure the success of future projects. I'm not sure I can honestly suggest that conflict is healthy. We had so much conflict on the Primo project, it wiped out the project's profitability. Some of the leaders barely speak to each other now."

"Hmm, that's not good at all. I'm guessing it got personal and became some kind of turf war, with egos involved."

"That's for sure," said Dave.

"The key to handling conflict is to make sure people understand it's okay to have an opposing view; however, it's important that the conflict doesn't become personal. If it does, that's when the leader needs to step in, stop the exchange, and get people back on track."

Dave nodded. "Do you have any tips on how to do that?"

"Sure. Keep focusing on the issue and the possible solutions. Make it clear that personal matters and preferences are to be kept out of the conversation, or at least to a minimum."

Dave looked at his notes again. A few pages down, he had begun creating a map of how the ideas linked together. The concept of collaboration wasn't simple. It was intertwined with many other aspects of working life. He needed to be clear about this in his report to Jim.

Beattie glanced at her watch. "Crikey, Dave, it's ten o'clock. We've left Dee alone for two hours! I came here to see my baby sister. Instead, I seem to be bonding with my Yankee brother-in-law," she said with a laugh.

On cue, Dee knocked gently on the door. "Hey, kids, I'm off to bed. All that beach time today has worn me out."

With Dee and Beattie heading off to sleep, Dave took advantage of the quiet to analyze Primo—the problems and the solutions—in light of what he'd learned about collaboration, the Heart domain, and the importance of asking for and sharing diverse perspectives. He went to his computer and began a document he could use as an outline for his report to Jim.

Issues Around the HEART Domain:

Utilizing Differences
Problems:

- To protect departmental silos, key talent was not shared by some department leaders.
- Insufficient diversity of perspective led to too much like-minded thinking and quick agreements, stifling innovation.
- Conflict was often personal, resulting in avoidance. Team members held back contributions and hesitated to push through potentially good ideas.

Solutions:

- Select group members based on talent and potential contribution rather than departmental preferences.
- Create an atmosphere that values diverse points of view.

- Perceive conflict as positive, creative, and issue driven. Don't allow personal attacks.
- Criteria for promotion should include a demonstrated ability to collaborate.

CHAPTER 5

Nurture Safety and Trust

The next day Dave once again joined Beattie in the kitchen for an early morning cup of coffee.

"This is becoming a habit," he said with a chuckle.

Beattie looked up and smiled. "How's Dee?"

"Still sleeping." Something that flickered across Beattie's face suggested there might be more behind the question. "Why?"

"Oh, nothing. I was so thrilled to feel the sun on my shoulders and my toes in the sand I was wondering if I'd overdone it with her yesterday."

Dave smiled. "I'm sure she'll recover."

"So what've you got on today, Dave?"

He looked at her blankly.

"At work?" she added with a smile, clarifying her British phrasing.

"Oh! I have a meeting first thing with Jim."

"Aha—perhaps I could quickly give you the second aspect of the Heart domain of collaboration."

"Second aspect—okay."

"Let me start by asking you: What do you think is the biggest barrier to people wanting to share their perspective?"

Dave thought for a while. "It could be lots of things, I guess. I think most people are a little afraid to stick their necks out, to be honest."

Beattie nodded. "You're right. People need to feel safe to be who they are—to speak up when they have an idea, or to speak out when they feel something isn't right. They also need to trust that they won't be punished if something goes wrong."

Dave thought about how a more trusting environment might have allowed for more participation and even changed the financial outcome of the Primo project.

Beattie continued. "Fear is a big inhibitor. Besides keeping people from speaking up, it also stops them from experimenting with an idea—and that's exactly what you need for innovation. We have a major job on our hands reprogramming people about this, because our educational systems have drummed it into us to always conform and never risk failure. This has built up an incredible collective memory, so we instinctively don't want to be different, make a mistake, or, worst of all, be singled out for blame."

"Hang on." Dave went to his briefcase and pulled out his notepad. He turned to a clean page and wrote *Create a safe and trusting environment.*

Beattie continued. "Nurturing an atmosphere of safety and trust allows people to act without fear of failure or retribution. In this environment, silos are minimized because trust becomes the bottom line. And at the risk of repeating myself, I would emphasize that it all begins with *you.*"

As Dave listened to Beattie, even though he knew he was part of the problem, he hoped the phrase "Collaboration begins with you" also applied to Jim. A chill ran across Dave's shoulders as he remembered Jim's words: *I need to do some thinking, too.* He dreaded this morning's meeting. *Here I am, fifty years old,* he thought, *and I actually have to summon the courage to talk to my boss. I've known him for years, but I'm worried if I tell him something he doesn't want to hear, it might get me fired.*

"Any questions?" Beattie asked. "You look concerned."

Dave got up from the table and refilled his coffee. "I was just thinking that nurturing a safe and trusting environment seems like a daunting task—and it doesn't seem to be one of my boss's strength areas."

"Think of it this way," suggested Beattie. "This could be an area where Jim could use your help. Establishing and nurturing safety and trust was one of the hardest aspects of our culture to change. It takes time. You have to approach it from both an organizational and an individual point of view, where it starts at the top and flows down to the leaders and then to the front line people. Convince Jim it's well worth his time. He needs to know that when people feel trusted they believe that the performance of the organization isn't just top management's responsibility—it's their responsibility, too."

They both stood up. "Thanks for your help, Beattie. I'll keep you posted."

***

Shortly after arriving at work, Dave took a deep breath and knocked on Jim's office door.

"Come on in," Jim called. As Dave walked in, Jim looked up briefly and motioned in the direction of a chair.

"Good morning," Dave said, doing his best to disguise his feelings of dread, even though he could hear Beattie's mantra, "Collaboration begins with you," ringing in his ears.

Jim flipped through the bound document in front of him and looked up at Dave with his eyebrows raised.

"Well, guess what?" he asked.

"What?"

"We won Primo II! Can you believe it? Despite the fact that Primo made absolutely no money for us, it seems the client was pleased with the end product."

Dave felt pleased and distressed at the same time.

"We pulled it off," Jim continued, "but we can't let Primo II be a repeat of Primo."

"I agree," said Dave.

"So how's that report on Primo coming along?"

"It's only been two days," said Dave. "I'm still gathering data."

"Okay, but I'd like to read your findings before we get too far into Primo II. We should incorporate any insights we get from your report, if we have the time."

"But if the past is any indication, we *won't* have the time, because we won't *make* the time," said Dave. "We're always moving forward at warp speed. We don't allow ourselves a few weeks or even days to analyze our past mistakes and learn from them. We're always chasing the next big contract, trying to learn and innovate at the same time, with everyone pulling in the direction of their own fiefdom."

Jim frowned. "Dave, I know I told you in our last meeting that it was your job to fix these kinds of problems. But since then, I've been doing a lot of thinking—and looking in the mirror. Although you're the lead on the Primo projects, improving the culture at Cobalt needs to start with me. At first I didn't like you being a truth teller, but now I have to admit that's what I need—maybe now more than ever before."

"What do you mean?"

Jim's voice softened. "This isn't for general broadcasting, but I've had some developments in my personal life that have caused me to—shall we say—*reevaluate* both my general temperament and my leadership style. A while ago my wife essentially told me that either I get rid of the 'my way or the highway attitude,' as she put it, or she would file for divorce. We've been in counseling for the past few weeks, and I'm beginning to see how that lousy attitude permeates everything I do, both at home and at work. And your recent comments have reinforced that."

"I think our wives went to the same school of truth telling. My wife told me just last night that I need to get my ego out of the way—to recognize my role in making things better, not spend all my time placing blame on others."

"Sounds like we're both in the middle of a personal learning process," said Jim.

"You know, the truth can sometimes hurt, but I'm sure we'll be better off if we take their advice," said Dave.

Jim cleared his throat. "Getting back to the subject at hand—in your analysis of Primo so far, have you gained any insights that might help us going forward with Primo II?"

"Well, I have been getting some excellent leadership coaching," Dave said.

"Who's your coach?"

"Her name's Beattie Anderson. She's from the UK, where she just sold her company—with very successful results."

"What kind of coaching is she giving you?" Jim asked.

"She's teaching me about the importance of collaboration in an organizational environment," said Dave, hopeful that Jim would be receptive.

"Okay, keep going," said Jim.

"I'm learning that collaboration is an inside-out mindset. It starts in the Heart, which is about who you are as a collaborator; then moves to the Head, which is what you believe about collaboration; and then goes to the Hands, which represent what you do during collaboration."

Jim gave Dave a skeptical look. "It sounds a little soft to me."

"It may seem that way, but she credits it for turning her company around and helping them beat the competition. One of the first things she told me is that applying the model in real life takes practice and time."

Jim sighed audibly. "Okay."

"The first key aspect of a collaborative heart is to realize you need to listen to different points of view. If you always get input from the same people—the ones who think the way you do—your output will become stale. Diversity is the source of innovation. There's an old saying that goes, 'If two people always agree, one of them is unnecessary.'"

Jim looked interested. "That's very true. But being successful in business isn't as easy as listening to opposing points of view. It takes guts and tenacity. Sometimes that requires making tough personnel decisions."

Dave shifted uneasily in his chair. *Tough personnel decisions.* Jim didn't seem to be very interested in creating a safe and trusting environment. Dave wondered, even with Jim's new insights into the problems with his old style, if he might still be looking for a fall guy for Primo. Yet if that happened, it would only perpetuate the blame culture everyone complained about while denying its existence. How was he going to tell that to Jim?

"Something on your mind, Dave?"

"Yes—there's a lot on my mind, actually," Dave blurted, surprising himself. "My coach said the second key aspect of collaboration is to create an environment where people can feel trusted and safe—safe to speak their truth and even share about their mistakes, so that we all can learn from each other."

Jim was silent for a moment.

"You know, that's probably a good point," said Jim. "Everybody really should be able to speak their minds without fear of punishment. If I penalize people for being truthful, they'll learn to cover up their mistakes and things might get out of hand. And if I ignore my wife's feedback, I might come home and find a moving van in front of my house."

Dave gulped. "I'm not sure what to say to that."

"It's all right, I've been having trouble coming up with the right words myself lately," said Jim. "At any rate, I want you to send me periodic drafts as you're working on your report about Primo. I think I'd like to get the truth a little bit at a time."

Dave took his cue and left. Closing the door, he silently congratulated himself for taking the first step toward creating a safe and trusting environment—and being a silo buster himself.

***

That afternoon Dave called his department heads and staff together to formally announce that Cobalt had secured the Primo II project. He also hoped, especially after the discussion with Jim, to begin the journey to collaboration—however bumpy the road might be.

Opening the door to the meeting room, Dave was hit with the din of two dozen people talking as they waited for the meeting to begin. The noise level gradually subsided as Dave made his way to the front of the room.

He greeted his audience with a smile. "Good afternoon, ladies and gentleman."

A man in the front row turned around to catch the eyes of the audience. "And any others," he quipped.

There were a few laughs and someone shouted out, "Speak for yourself, Wayne."

Based on his experience working with Wayne Lundgren, Dave knew it was typical for him to be disruptive. He'd been in the research and development department for over fifteen years and was now the senior manager. His ability to develop big-dollar programs made people tolerant of his less-than-ideal behavior. Self-serving and egotistical, he liked his own way and always made sure he and his team came out on top. He certainly did not operate from a collaborative mindset.

Dave decided he would keep his focus on his audience and cleared his throat.

"This is going to be a quick meeting," he began. "By now you may have heard through the Cobalt grapevine that we've won Primo II."

Everyone cheered.

"But it was at a huge cost," Dave continued. "We took a loss on Primo. I'm sure Jim—and our stockholders—aren't going to stand for a repeat of that. I've been doing a post-project analysis and, after looking at the data, it's clear we could have saved money by combining departmental efforts. In many ways we operated in self-serving silos—and that has to change for Primo II. Cobalt is *our* company. Whatever we do, we need to do it for the common good." He looked directly at Wayne. "That means making a profit for the company as a whole, not just for our own departments."

Wayne let out an audible yawn.

Dave focused again on the rest of the room. "We're going to approach Primo II with a new strategy. Rather than working as independent entities—which costs us time and money—I want all departments represented in this room to start collaborating. In the next couple of weeks, you're going to hear the word *collaboration* a lot. Here's something that will help the idea start sinking in."

He walked over to the flip chart at the front of the room and, with a dramatic flourish, tore off the cover sheet to reveal:

Collaboration Begins with YOU

- Collaboration is an inside-out mindset
- Heart ☐ Head ☐ Hands: The 3 Domains of Collaboration
- The heart is **who you are** as a collaborator
- Effective collaborators know the importance of **listening to different perspectives** and **creating a safe and trusting environment**

Dave said, "These are some of the phrases and concepts we'll be learning and living as we work together to create a culture of collaboration at Cobalt. Today we'll familiarize ourselves with the Heart domain. I'll be rolling out the Head and Hands domains over the next several days. For now I want you to focus on the last point. We will begin holding periodic idea sessions this week where *everyone* will be encouraged to contribute suggestions and thoughts. I want you all to know you can feel safe to speak up at these sessions. We really want to hear from you."

Some of the newer hires smiled and murmured quietly to each other.

Sarah spoke up. "I'm excited about this. I think creating a collaborative culture could be the beginning of a new era at Cobalt where everybody's perspective is considered."

"I agree with Sarah," said Dave. "And for those of you who, like Sarah, technically aren't leaders here at Cobalt—yet—I want you to start thinking of yourselves as important contributors. I'll be talking more about that as we go along."

By this time, Wayne had slumped in his chair, his head resting on his palm, the picture of boredom. Dave couldn't go on ignoring this.

"Speaking of different perspectives—Wayne, do you have anything to share with the group?"

"Yes, I have a question."

"Great! What's your question?"

"How much longer is this meeting going to last?"

"Patience is a virtue, Wayne. The second point under the Heart domain is to create a safe and trusting environment. This is vital in order for collaboration to take place. We need great ideas—but until everyone feels safe speaking up, we won't get those ideas."

Brandon Savedra, a member of the production department, raised his hand.

"Brandon, go ahead," said Dave.

"Sometimes I have an idea but I don't want to bring it up because I think someone will disagree with it or say it's bad. How can we feel safe to express our opinions and ideas if we know someone else—maybe a manager—might not like them?"

"Disagreement can actually be healthy as long as we're dealing with conflicting *ideas,* not conflicting *people.* It's okay to respectfully debate ideas, but it's not okay for things to get personal. If conflict happens, as leader of the project I'll take an active role in helping to reach a positive resolution."

Dave saw heads nodding. "So when you're in a group that's sharing ideas, remember to listen with respect and suspend judgment. That's the starting point for trust. We'll have a policy that there's no such thing as a bad idea. When people feel trusted, they'll begin to understand they are contributors—and we'll get great ideas and happy people. As we move forward with Primo II, let's welcome our differences rather than shying away from them. Act with integrity and show you care about each other. Think of it this way: none of us is as smart as all of us."

People started closing notebooks and getting ready to leave.

"Before the next meeting, I need each of you to email me with the resources you'll need to deliver Primo II. I also want you to document the lessons you learned from Primo—both good and bad. The sooner the better on this. I'd like everyone's initial thoughts by tomorrow morning. We'll reconvene tomorrow afternoon to continue the launch."

***

At six o'clock Dave wrapped things up at the office and made his way home to Dee and Beattie. Pulling up to the house, he saw a lone light shining in the living room window and immediately sensed something was wrong. When he walked through the front door, the house was quiet. He dropped his briefcase in his office and made his way to the living room, where Dee and Beattie were sitting together.

"Hi, girls—what's going on?"

Dee gave her husband a tight smile. "Sit down, honey. I have something to tell you."

His heart stopped and restarted in an instant. He took a sharp breath and felt his muscles tense. Beattie placed a steadying hand on Dee's arm.

"I have to go the hospital next week for a surgical biopsy."

"What?" said Dave, stunned.

"There's a possibility—I might have breast cancer." Dee's eyes filled with tears.

After the word was spoken, a quiet sadness filled the room. Dave sank into the sofa next to his wife and held her in his arms as she wept. Beattie slipped out for a walk to gather her thoughts.

CHAPTER 6

Involve Others in Crafting a Clear Purpose, Values, and Goals

Dave kissed Dee gently so as not to wake her and quietly headed into the kitchen. The sun was not up, but there was enough light to see that it would rise into a cloudy sky. When he arrived in the kitchen, Dave wasn't surprised to see Beattie already nursing her tea.

"Sleep much?" she asked.

"Not at all," Dave said. "Dee, on the other hand, is out like a light."

"She's emotionally exhausted. My poor sister." Beattie took a sip of her tea. "Would you mind terribly joining me on a walk this morning? I need to talk this out."

"Sure. Let me grab a pair of shoes."

They spent the first twenty minutes talking about Dee—sharing fears and hopes as well as what Beattie had read about the latest medical technologies.

"I guess there's really not much we can do at this point but wait—and be as supportive as possible," said Beattie as they rounded a corner and headed back toward the house.

"I realize that. It's just that I wish I could take some kind of action," said Dave. "I get anxious when I'm powerless."

"I understand," said Beattie. After a moment, she changed the subject. "Want to talk about how things are at the office?"

"Things aren't too bad," Dave admitted. "Surprisingly, despite the fact that it was a dud profit-wise, the Primo product was good enough that we scored Primo II."

"That's the first good news I've heard all week," said Beattie, smiling. "Congratulations."

"Thanks, but don't congratulate me too soon. If we don't turn things around, Primo II will be another money pit, and my job could be in jeopardy." Dave sighed. "Given what's going on with Dee, that's the last thing I need."

"Don't go there. Let's stay focused on solutions," said Beattie as they turned up the front steps.

"I called an all-department meeting yesterday and introduced everyone to the idea of collaboration. And I taught them about the Heart domain and the importance of listening to diverse opinions and establishing safety and trust. My new ally, Sarah, modeled it all by speaking up and supporting me."

"Good for her!" said Beattie.

Back in the kitchen, Dave showed Beattie his notes, including the problems and solutions he had identified around safety and trust at Cobalt:

Issues Around the HEART Domain:

Safety and Trust
Problems:
- Ideas were often criticized or dismissed, resulting in low levels of trust.
- Politics and silos negatively affected the project as department managers sought to maintain control with minimal involvement.
- Some were reluctant to volunteer or share ideas for fear of antagonizing their boss.
- We have a blame culture where people are disciplined for mistakes. We should see mistakes as learning opportunities.

Solutions:
- Make safety and trust a value.
- Train leaders in behaviors that promote trust and respect. Bust existing silos and focus on what's best for the project.
- Suspend judgment and decisions until all ideas have been heard.
- Reward collaboration.
- Allow people to learn from experiments and encourage creative problem solving and innovation.

"That's a good start," said Beattie.

"What's troubling me now," Dave said, "is that I have no idea how to launch Primo II in a collaborative way."

"Then it's time to move to the Head domain. That's all about what you know—your beliefs and attitudes about collaboration," said Beattie.

"Fire away," said Dave with a smile, scribbling on his note pad.

"Most people don't realize there are two parts to collaborative leadership: vision/direction and implementation. Vision/direction is about going somewhere. If people don't know where you want them to go, what's the chance they'll ever get there?"

"Zero," admitted Dave.

"Right," said Beattie. "For example, if you don't make it clear that it's safe for people to share their best ideas, they may hold back out of a need to protect themselves."

"So whose responsibility is it to make sure vision and direction are clear?" asked Dave.

"What do you think?"

"I think it must be the leader's responsibility," said Dave. "It's mine for Primo II and Jim's for the whole company."

"Exactly. It's the leader's responsibility to set the vision and direction. It's important that others contribute to crafting the vision, but it's up to the leader to make sure it's set in stone."

"How do you get people to act on it?" asked Dave.

"That's where implementation comes in. That's when people become responsible, empowered contributors, and the leader's job is to be responsive in helping them live according to the vision and direction and accomplish the goals. We'll get to implementation later, when we talk about the Hands domain."

"Okay. So right now we're talking about vision and direction."

"Yes. And what really defined the vision and drove results at Blenheim was when we developed a common purpose, values, and goals. A clear purpose unites everyone around a common objective, values guide behavior, and goals provoke action—but only when the entire organization has a chance to contribute."

"How did you do it?" asked Dave.

"Our top management took the first shot at it. They developed a draft purpose statement, a set of operating values, and strategic goals. Then they shared their draft throughout the organization, asking people what they liked and what they thought was missing from the proposal in order for them to engage with it and feel a sense of ownership."

"They really asked everyone's opinion?"

"Absolutely," said Beattie. "People have a hard time committing to something if they've had no involvement."

"There's a learning right there," said Dave. "Jim introduced a mission statement and values at Cobalt a while ago, but it was a top-down implementation. If you ask anyone today what our mission or values are, I guarantee they will shrug their shoulders. I agree with what you're saying: when people aren't involved in creating mission and values statements, psychologically they just stick them in a drawer and forget about them. I certainly don't see our values reflected in anyone's behavior. And regardless of what a plaque on the wall says, from the way people behave, you'd think Cobalt's one and only mission is to make money."

Dave thought about Wayne and his team. Some of them acted like wannabe Waynes, emulating his power broker style of leadership.

"We have a top-down, tough-guy culture that doesn't focus on so-called soft skills like collaboration," he said.

"We did, too," said Beattie. "And that culture was suppressing hidden stores of talent and energy at Blenheim. Our leadership finally realized that the top-down naming of a clear purpose, values, and goals wouldn't cut it—our people needed to have a part in it. Only when we involved everyone did they take our purpose seriously and make sure our values were clearly communicated and supported by company policies and leader behavior. That's when our macho culture gave way to something far more powerful."

***

That afternoon in the meeting room, Dave had just finished arranging the tables and chairs so people could sit in small groups. He was setting up the flip chart when he heard a voice.

"Would you like me to rearrange the room so we can all sit around one table?"

Dave looked up to see Steve Frazier, the newest member of Wayne's team. Dave appreciated Steve's willingness to help. Evidently, he hadn't been tainted yet by Wayne's dog-eat-dog leadership style.

"Thanks for the offer, Steve. Actually, I'm trying something new to see if I can get people to interact more. What do you think?"

"I like that idea," said Steve with a smile. He then selected a seat at the table farthest from the front.

Dave thought Steve's seating choice revealed a classic need for safety. *Perhaps Wayne's gotten to him after all,* he thought.

Several more people came in, including Wayne, who took a look at the tables and said, "Hey, what do you know? We're gonna have party games this afternoon!"

A few people snickered. Wayne and Dave had been peers before Dave's promotion to vice president a few years ago, and Dave still wasn't comfortable dealing with his boorish behavior. Wayne would always do whatever he could to disrupt meetings and get things on his terms. *I can no longer let that happen if I'm going to accept my role as a silo buster,* thought Dave.

More people came into the room until every seat was filled. As Dave stood at the front, an expectant silence came over the attendees.

"Hi, everyone," Dave began. "Thanks for sending me the resources you'll need for Primo II and your thoughts on where we fell short with Primo. I'll be sharing some of those with the group today."

Wayne spoke without raising his hand. "Do we really need to do all that? If my department gets involved with Primo II—and that's a big *if* at this point—I already know what resources we need and how to get them. And it wasn't *my* department that fell short with Primo. I'd like to just get on with what the company has hired us to do."

This comment was over the top. Dave knew he couldn't let Wayne's disruption stand and instantly saw a way to turn the situation to his own advantage.

"I'm glad you brought up those points, Wayne, because they highlight what's going to be different about this project. As I said in our meeting yesterday, we're taking a new approach with Primo II. The emphasis will be on collaboration. So to answer your question, yes, we really *do* need to 'do all that'—to share with the group what went wrong last time and to brainstorm new ways of working together."

No one spoke, but Dave saw several smiles around the room.

"One of the problems we had with Primo," he continued, "is that although we looked like a project group, we were really working in silos—only sharing information when it was absolutely necessary. It was more like forced cooperation than collaboration."

He uncovered a new page on the flip chart, which read:

> • The head is **what you know:** your beliefs and attitudes about collaboration
> • A successful project begins with a **clear purpose, values, and goals**

"With Primo, we were missing the main ingredient under the Head domain. We didn't have a clear purpose, values, and goals for the project—and that was my responsibility. We should have put our heads together to figure out where our project was going and what would guide our journey. A clear purpose will unite us as we move forward, values will guide our behavior, and goals will focus our energy."

Wayne groaned loudly. "My only goal is to make money, not sit around talking about purpose and values. Besides, Cobalt already has a purpose and values."

"Good point." Dave challenged Wayne with a smile. "What are they?"

Wayne hesitated. "Something about being innovative and successful."

Around the room a few heads nodded.

"That's close," said Dave. "Cobalt's stated purpose is 'to keep our industry moving forward by innovating for success.'" He wrote the phrase on the flip chart.

"At your tables, I want you to work on a new purpose statement for Primo II that aligns with Cobalt's purpose statement. I'll give you about ten minutes. After everyone reports out, we'll work on our values and goals."

The room buzzed with conversation.

When ten minutes was up, Dave had each group report their suggested purpose statement. After a vigorous discussion, the group settled on the purpose of Primo II: "To keep our company moving forward by innovating for success."

"Excellent!" said Dave as he wrote the new purpose statement on the flip chart. "That's a great start. Now, let's move to values. Can anyone remember any of Cobalt's values?"

"Success," came the first reply.

"Relationships," came another. Both met with murmurs of agreement.

"Good—that's two," said Dave. "In fact, Cobalt has four rank-ordered values." Dave turned to a fresh sheet and wrote:

---

1. Integrity—Do the right thing

2. Relationships—Build mutual trust and respect with our people, our customers, our suppliers, and our community

> **3.** Success—Contribute to the growth and prosperity of our company
> **4.** Learning—Continue to get better

"How do you like these four values?" he said to the group. "Should we keep them for Primo II, should we change one or two, or should we establish a whole different set? Talk about it at your tables for a few minutes and see what you come up with." Again the room was filled with noisy enthusiasm as everyone started sharing their thoughts.

Dave soon pulled the whole group together to get their feedback. The consensus for Primo II was to keep the first three rank-ordered values but change the fourth value from *Learning* to *Creativity.*

"I think Creativity is a great fourth value for Primo II—particularly because it's what will drive the innovation our client is looking for."

Dave continued. "Now let's zero in on the Success value for a minute. I think with Primo, we focused so much on achieving our departmental goals that the success of the project took a back seat. So back to your point, Wayne: you and your team may have a goal of making money, but that could actually be detrimental to Primo II's Success value."

Anthony Tate, one of Wayne's team members, raised a hand and Dave pointed to him.

"How could our department making money be detrimental to success?" the young man asked. "I don't get it."

"Excellent question," said Dave. "To answer that, I'll share some feedback I got in response to my question about what didn't work with Primo. As we can tell by the client's decision to give us the Primo II contract, the product itself was innovative and brilliant. That certainly satisfies our new Creativity value."

Wayne, whose department had developed the prototype, stood up and took a dramatic bow. There was a polite smattering of applause.

Lisa Virani, head of the production department, raised her hand. "Mind if I say something?"

"Sure, Lisa," said Dave, eager to get Lisa's input.

"Wayne, in some ways, your department's focus on its own profit not only kept you from making necessary contributions but actually interfered with the overall success of the project. We really needed your involvement—but because true collaboration, as Dave has been describing it, wasn't happening, Primo's development was behind schedule early on. My department missed some key deadlines. This led to a series of overtime expenses and rush charges, which affected not only our budget but also those of at least three other departments."

Dave stepped in. "Thanks, Lisa." He turned to Wayne. "So Wayne, while your department might have met its benchmark and showed a profit, the company overall took a loss. Even though the client liked the product, Primo didn't live up to Cobalt's Success value."

People shifted in their seats. This kind of straight talk was unusual at Cobalt and clearly was making some people uncomfortable.

"Now, wait a minute," Wayne began.

Dave held up his hand. "Here's the thing. I'm absolutely not here to point fingers. I was the lead VP on Primo, so if there's any blame to be assigned, it belongs to me for not making our purpose and values clear so we could all get on the same page. The reason we're doing this now is so that we can pull together to create a better outcome with Primo II. Now, are there any questions?"

At the back of the room, the new software engineer, Steve Frazier, raised his hand.

"What you've been describing sounds to me like a conflict between our Creativity value and our Success value. How does that get resolved if I'm developing a product that's amazingly creative and innovative, but that may lead to cost overages?"

"Another great question!" said Dave. "The values are ranked 1 through 4, in order of importance. As you can see, Creativity is ranked number 4 behind Integrity, Relationships, and Success. That means if your creative effort is going to undermine the financial success of our project, it's a no-go. Likewise, you don't want your creative effort to harm any relationships or undermine the project's integrity. The other three values come first."

Wayne rocked back in his chair and folded his arms. "Okay, let's be done. I need to get out of here."

Dave was tempted to tell Wayne he was more than welcome to leave. But he knew that Wayne's help in making resources available was critical to developing Primo II. If Wayne didn't buy into this approach, Dave would be back where he started—or worse.

"We still need to settle on our key goals for Primo II. Back to your table conversations, everyone—see if you can identify three or four key goals that, if accomplished, will make the Primo II project a real winner."

After the group spent several minutes brainstorming among their table teams, Dave pulled them back together again and summarized in a bulleted list on the flip chart the four key goals that had emerged from the discussion.

"It looks like we've all settled on our four key goals going forward." The page read:

Key Goals

- Cobalt makes a significant profit on Primo II.

> - The collaboration process modeled by the Primo II project team has a major positive effect on the organization as a whole.
> - Everyone participating in Primo II feels fully engaged and valued for their contributions.
> - The client loves the product so much, Cobalt is given a contract for Primo III.

"Good work, people!" said Dave, and began to applaud. Within seconds, everyone in the room had joined in—even Wayne.

Dave beamed. "Thanks for your work on this. We're going to stop now, but I want you to email me any further thoughts or reactions you have about our work today. I want this to continue to be a group effort among all the departments represented here. I appreciate your time, everyone."

The room cleared quickly. As Dave started straightening up the tables, his thoughts went to Dee. The challenges of the day had given him a welcome reprieve from worrying about her cancer threat. Now his anxieties came flooding back. *What if she does have cancer? What if she has to have a mastectomy? What if she dies?*

"Hey, need a hand?"

Dave turned to see Sarah gathering up a few stray papers and pens.

"You okay?" she asked.

"Sure, fine," Dave fibbed. "Why do you ask?"

"You look pretty upset."

As they walked back to their offices, Dave shared the news about Dee.

"That's tough, Dave," said Sarah. "I'll keep your wife in my prayers."

***

In his office that afternoon, Dave captured for his report his thoughts on what he'd learned about the Head domain, crafting a clear purpose, values, and goals, and how it all applied to Primo II.

Issues Around the HEAD Domain:

Establishing a Clear Purpose, Values, and Goals

Problems:

• Lack of clarity about the purpose of the project

• No clear values to guide decision making

• Goals not clear

• No value placed on collaboration

• Too much value placed on short-term results

Solutions:

• Together, clarify the purpose of the Primo II project

- Together, establish clear values to guide decision making
- Together, set specific goals to focus everyone's behavior
- Encourage and support collaboration
- Ensure that results support the company's and project's purpose

CHAPTER 7

A Step Backward

That night Beattie cooked dinner, and the three of them talked about Dee's health. Dave couldn't understand why Dee had kept her fears to herself. He shared that he had felt a little excluded—that to him it was almost as if the sisters had decided this was a woman's problem and had closed ranks on him. Dee assured him that wasn't the case and that she would be completely open with him going forward.

"To be honest, I'm really at a loss," Dave confessed. "I don't know what to do or say."

"You're doing fine, honey," said Dee, patting his hand.

He didn't say it out loud, but Dave was scared. His thoughts ricocheted in his mind: *Am I going to be the man she needs me to be? What does she need? Will I be able to care for her? How much time off from work will I need? Primo II will have to wait!*

Dave did his best to lighten up for the rest of the evening. As bedtime approached, they all decided they needed a nightcap. Dee retired first.

Dave sensed Beattie wanted to talk. *And hell, yes,* he thought, *I want to know why my sister-in-law—a woman I haven't seen in years—suddenly turns up and is now my wife's new best friend.*

"How did Primo II go today, Dave?"

"Primo again. Is that all you can think about?" Dave exclaimed.

"Of course not!" Beattie matched his tone and volume.

"Tell me, Beattie, why was I the last to know about this? How come you just happen to be here when my wife gets cancer?"

"Dave, we don't know if she has cancer. And I didn't know before I came—I didn't know a thing until she told me the day we went to the beach that she had found a tiny lump. I made her call and make an appointment immediately. Luckily, she could be seen right away."

He sighed. "I just don't understand why she told you first."

"I don't think she knew what to do. I just happened to be here. With me being her big sis and all, I suppose the universe threw everything together and she told me. The important thing is that she's doing something about it."

"I guess you're right," said Dave. He was exhausted.

They drained their glasses in unison and called it a night. Neither slept well.

***

Dave had already boiled the water for Beattie's tea the next morning when she walked into the kitchen, still wearing her robe and slippers.

"Sorry I was such a jerk last night," he said.

Beattie shrugged. "It's okay. We're all feeling it. The biopsy is Monday."

"You're right. I guess worrying won't help. I hate to say it, but maybe talking about my project will be a good distraction."

"Sure," said Beattie. "First tell me how it went yesterday with your group."

Dave recounted the successes of the day: the success of the table group activities and the contributions from Lisa, Steve, and Anthony.

"Sounds like you're cultivating a few new silo busters! I also love the fact the meeting wasn't all about you because of the way you involved everyone in decision making. How was Wayne's behavior?"

"He attempted to be disruptive as usual, but I think I managed to turn lemons into lemonade this time."

"You know, for all his bluster, Wayne is probably insecure," Beattie noted.

Dave let out a laugh. "Wayne, insecure? Hardly. He's one of the most egotistical guys I know."

"Exactly," said Beattie. "Whenever you see someone flaunting their superiority, you know they're a scared little kid inside because their ego is feeling threatened. It's hard to make other people feel good about themselves and what they're doing if you don't feel good about yourself."

"What can I possibly do about that?" asked Dave.

"You need to build Wayne up, make him feel safe, and win his trust. That gets back to the Heart domain. Keep listening to him and try not to be defensive or judgmental. Let's talk for a minute about the Primo II project group. How different are they from the original Primo group?"

"Well, essentially it's the same cross-departmental team. And before you say anything—yes, I know they didn't deliver."

Beattie smiled. "So?"

"So in the spirit of 'Collaboration begins with you,' I've already begun to introduce some changes. As I told you, I'm making sure everyone gets a chance to contribute their thoughts this time. We need Wayne on the team, but he needs to allow his people to do more. I'm excited that two people in his department, Sarah and Steve, have already begun to speak up—they have great ideas. The problem is, Wayne has always had a pattern of shooting down their suggestions as soon as they're mentioned. He needs to get over that. He has a tendency to think that all good ideas start with him."

"So what are you going to do about him?"

"I don't know yet. We need him, that's for sure. He's brilliant and he's damn good at recruiting—I'm finding out his team has some of the brightest people at Cobalt. But he's prickly. I don't much like him, and I find it hard to trust him."

"I hear you," Beattie said, taking a serious tone. "But because you need him, you're going to have to figure out a way to build him up. And if you end up in conflict with each other, just remember: conflict is healthy—as long as you keep to the issues. If you feel you need it, ask for outside help to make that relationship work. You both have valuable experience and knowledge, so it'll be worth it."

Dave looked doubtful. "I'll do my best."

***

Later that day, Dave knocked on Wayne's door. *Here goes nothing,* he thought.

"Yeah!" he heard Wayne call out.

Dave stepped in the room and gave Wayne a stiff smile. "Hey—what did you think of the meeting yesterday?"

"Not much." Wayne seemed to be warming up for combat. He rocked back in his chair, simultaneously lifting his feet up onto his desk and putting his hands behind his head.

Wow, that was like a sit-up, but for the office rather than the gym! Dave thought. He was annoyed already—but then he remembered Beattie's advice.

"Wayne, I really need your help on Primo II. I want to talk about getting some support from you and your team to make this project succeed."

"Yep."

"For starters, we're going to need a couple of your team members full-time in the initial phases."

"Hang on a minute there." Wayne sat up straight, muscles tense, like a snake coiling to defend its territory. "I have other projects besides these money-sucking Primo fiascos, you know. And I'd rather my people work on jobs that are making a profit. My career is not going down the drain, Dave, and you might want to think carefully about your own. I see Primo II as a career-limiting project, and I plan to stay away."

Sensing this to be his best opening, Dave plunged in. "Wayne, I don't agree, given the purpose, values, and goals we all worked to establish in yesterday's meeting. This will only be a money-sucking fiasco if you turn your back on the things we agreed on and keep hoarding information and preventing your good people from sharing their ideas."

Wayne just laughed and shook his head without bothering to answer.

"Come on, Wayne, give your team a chance to shine and give Cobalt a chance to make a profit on Primo II. You hold the keys. We really need you."

With a smug look on his face, Wayne replied, "I'll think it over and let you know." He waved his fingers at Dave dismissively. "Now if you don't mind, I have a profit to make. Success is my number *one* value."

Dave's face was set in a grimace as he headed back to his office. He encountered Sarah in the hallway.

"Is that steam coming out of your ears?" she joked.

"As my dear sister-in-law would say, 'You're bloody right it is!'"

"I used to think British people were so prim and proper," Sarah said with a laugh. "They really aren't, are they? So what's the problem?"

Dave wanted to shout *The problem is Wayne!* but he played down his true feelings.

"I'm having a little trouble getting everybody on board with Primo II."

"Everybody? Such as?"

He had no intention of talking behind Wayne's back. For one thing, it would be a very effective way to blow whatever shred of safety and trust that might exist between them.

"Let's just leave it at that," said Dave.

"Don't forget what you told us yesterday about conflict being healthy."

Sarah's statement took Dave by surprise. After a moment of reflection, he said, "Thanks for reminding me. People aren't the problem—their behavior just gets in the way sometimes. Implementing collaboration isn't supposed to be an easy process. My coach keeps telling me 'Collaboration starts with *you*'—so right now, my focus needs to be on patience and persistence."

"I understand the patience part, but what do you mean about persistence?"

"I might have to be like a third grade teacher and keep telling everyone about collaboration over and over and over again, until they get it right, right, right!"

"Good luck, silo buster!" Sarah said with a smile.

"Thanks," said Dave, turning into his office as Sarah continued walking down the hall.

As Dave sat down at his desk, he could almost feel a change in his heart toward Wayne. The project needed him, and telling him what to do wasn't going to work. It was time to get strategic.

He crafted an email that would make the case to Wayne for the use of his team members. He clearly outlined the role each person would play, why the project needed them, and how important their contributions would be to making Primo II profitable while demonstrating the other agreed-upon project values of integrity, relationships, and creativity.

Feeling hopeful the email would win Wayne's support, Dave began the first draft of his report for Jim. He first wrote up Primo's results and then listed the reasons the project failed to make a profit. At the top of his list was managers withholding talent and information. With his change of heart, he decided not to name names as he knew it might present Wayne's head for the chopping block.

Faults with Primo I:

- Information was withheld or not fully shared.
- Some leaders exercised top-down control, calling the shots for their people and departments and then pulling people off the project with little notice.
- Group members gave priority to other duties instead of the project.
- Everything was rushed—no time for experimentation or innovation.
- Conflict was usually personal, not issue focused.

- Some leaders supported a blame culture where mistakes were not acceptable, which stifled good ideas and innovation.
- The purpose, values, and goals of Primo weren't made clear and therefore didn't get buy-in from group members.
- Little trust between group members and leaders led to reluctance of group members to voice opinions or ideas.

> • There was a scarcity of networking among departments.

Dave read over the list and then wrote at the bottom:

> • The solution: Develop a collaborative culture within the Primo II project group—and ultimately within the whole organization.

Dave emailed Jim the first draft of the report. He also sent Wayne a meeting request for Monday morning at 11:00 to talk about the report, attaching the first draft for him to read as well. Dave reasoned that if Wayne felt more included in this process, he might begin to see the importance of collaboration and therefore be more likely to get on board for Primo II.

CHAPTER 8

Talk Openly

Dave awoke early Monday morning with Dee in his arms. His first thought was how much he wished he could protect her. It felt terrible to have no power over what was to come.

Beattie and Dave grabbed a quick breakfast before they all left for the hospital. Even though the biopsy was outpatient surgery, Dee was prohibited from eating beforehand.

Seeing a hospital employee standing near the curb, Dave pulled up in front of the hospital entrance. "My wife is here for an outpatient procedure. Could you please tell me where I should park?" he asked the man.

"Glad you stopped. I'll take your bride in right now to meet our concierge. You can park wherever you'd like and then meet her on the third floor in the outpatient area."

"Concierge?" said Dave, surprised to hear the word used to describe a hospital employee.

"Absolutely," said the man. "We do everything we can to take exceptional care of our patients."

With that said, Dee hopped out of the car and walked into the hospital with the attendant. After Dave parked, he and Beattie found their way to the outpatient unit, where a charming middle-aged woman named Margery introduced herself as the concierge. She had already been ushering Dee around, checking her in and placing an ID band on her wrist. Margery smiled at Dave and Beattie and said, "Time for hugs and kisses, folks. Then we'll need you to wait in the family area down the hall. I'll come and get you when she's in recovery."

Dee turned to Dave. "Honey, I know you have a meeting with one of your department managers this morning. There's no point in you hanging around. It's not like I'm having brain surgery."

"I'm prepared to postpone that meeting. This is far more important."

Dee wouldn't hear of it. "Dave, go. Please. Beattie will keep me entertained."

"I promise I'll call when she's out of surgery," Beattie said.

Dave kissed his wife goodbye and forced a confident smile.

"See you in a bit," he said. "I know you're in good hands."

"She certainly is," said Margery warmly.

***

Dave had scheduled the meeting with Wayne in one of the company meeting rooms. He thought neutral territory might be better for them both.

"Thanks for taking the time for a quick meeting, Wayne. Did you have a chance to take a look at the draft of my report?"

"I skimmed it," said Wayne. "You know, Dave, the reason I don't 'collaborate,' as you call it, is that I get paid on my department's accomplishments. My people and I get paid on what we do. It's a no-brainer. I focus on what we get paid on."

"*Only* what you get paid on?"

"Occasionally I focus on other things," Wayne said.

"Such as?"

"Stuff that gets me promoted—simple as that."

Curious and thinking how to capture this in his report, Dave probed deeper. "So what does that mean, exactly?"

"That means not focusing on dumb projects that will lose money and make me look bad," Wayne said with a laugh.

"So your first condition for working on Primo II would be to get paid for it—then you'd do it?"

"If I got paid outright? Yeah, in that case I'd probably do it."

Dave frowned. He wanted to shout out "Mercenary!" but restrained himself. This change of heart was challenging. *But I need Wayne, so I have to find a way to compensate him somehow.*

"Okay, Wayne, I hear you. I'll work on the money piece and get back to you. Keep in mind that if this project goes right, it will mean the start of a lot more follow-up projects that will need to be led by someone who knows how to collaborate and bring things in on budget. That could be career enhancing for you."

With that, Dave ended the meeting and headed back to his office. He hoped Wayne would think about the meaning behind his words. *Wayne has to realize that if he doesn't want to put his own job in jeopardy, he needs Primo II to succeed as much as the rest of us do.*

Dave no sooner sat down at his desk than he received a text from Beattie: "She's in recovery. All went well. Should be able to go home in an hour or two."

***

Dave made his way through the outpatient unit to Dee's bedside in the recovery area. As he approached the bed, he could see her shifting position although her eyes were still closed.

"She's beginning to stir a bit now," Beattie whispered. "The nurse said everything went fine and pathology results will take a few days. Hopefully, you'll hear something by Friday."

Dave kissed his fingertips, placed them gently on Dee's lips, and waited for her to wake up and be cleared to head home.

***

The following morning Beattie was in the kitchen working on her laptop as Dave scuffed in, going straight for the coffee.

"How'd our girl do last night?" Beattie asked.

"Slept like a rock." He poured himself a cup, added sugar, and stirred. "Me, not so much. I want it to be Friday so we all know what she's got to deal with."

"We both know how strong she is," said Beattie. "Let's try not to worry until we have something to worry about."

Dave smiled. He looked at Beattie's laptop and mimicked one of her Britishisms. "So what've you got on today?"

Beattie smiled. "Just checking my email. I suppose I could've been back at the office by now, but my sister's health is more important. Besides, I think you could use my help for a little longer, too."

"Thanks," said Dave. "It's great having you here."

"My business—correction, *the* business—is in safe hands, anyway. After the company was sold I became chairman of the board, so I'll still be hanging around for a few years in that role. They don't need me for the day-to-day stuff anymore. But, dear God," she said, scrolling through multiple screens of email, "they do like to keep me informed!"

"That sounds like a good problem to have."

"I suppose so. I'd rather know what's going on than not."

"That's one of the primary problems we need to work on at Cobalt," said Dave. "People tend to hold information close to the vest. They use it like currency, as though making it scarce will drive up its value."

"Oh, that's not good," said Beattie. "Communication is the lifeblood of an organization and central to the Hands domain—what you do as a collaborator. Without communication, you can't implement your vision or purpose and your company can die. In fact, open communication is one of the key parts of the Hands domain."

"Great—tell me about it," said Dave as he pulled his notepad out of his briefcase.

"As a collaborative leader, you support people in their work—you remove roadblocks and help them win. You communicate openly by being a real-time coach: praising people's progress when they're living according to the purpose and values and achieving goals, and gently redirecting their efforts when they get off course. When people realize they're in a safe and supportive environment, they feel they can also talk openly—candidly—and true collaboration happens."

"Well, I did talk openly with Wayne yesterday. I was quite candid."

Beattie's eyebrows shot up. "And?"

"The bottom line is that he thinks Primo II will be another financial loser, and therefore he doesn't want to have a thing to do with it."

"He won't work on the project at all?"

"Not unless he gets paid to work on it."

"Actually, that's terrific to know," said Beattie without a trace of sarcasm.

Dave looked at her with disbelief. "Seriously?"

"Seriously. First, you're to be commended for talking openly and getting down to the facts of what's going on with Wayne. There's an old saying: 'The facts are friendly.'"

"Even bad news facts?"

"Yes, even bad news facts. The idea is that no matter how disagreeable the facts may be, they lead you closer to what's really going on. Denial of a problem doesn't make it go away."

"So I should *thank* Wayne for being a profit monger?"

"Of course not. I'm just saying that communicating his concern could be the first step to fixing something that's wrong. When communication uncovers breakdowns or failures, it can be a good thing. Maybe this issue with Wayne is an opportunity for your leadership team and HR to review the compensation structure. This might not just be a problem for him—he may unknowingly be speaking on behalf of others in the company."

"You have a good point."

"But let's get back to your conversation. By listening to understand rather than to argue, you were able to get some vital information about what makes him tick. That's what the company needs—more shared information."

"But isn't there some information that shouldn't be shared?" asked Dave.

"The idea that some company information should be limited to a select few is generally not productive. People who are fully informed make better decisions. When you keep certain information behind closed doors, you limit people's ability to see the big picture and act accordingly. It sabotages any notion of empowerment. And when people don't know what's going on, it's human nature for them to fill in the blanks and imagine a version that's ten times worse than the truth!

"For example," Beattie continued, "our company went through a tough period during the last recession. So before rumors started flying, we opened our books and shared our situation properly with our people. After all, we were all in it together—our lives at that point were inextricably linked to each other. So we told them what was what and encouraged everyone to share their ideas for increasing income and cutting expenses. Surprisingly, this process actually strengthened our organization in the face of adversity. Instead of cutting staff and demoralizing those who were left, we talked openly, restored profits, and earned one another's loyalty."

"I can't see Jim sharing sensitive information like that," Dave said doubtfully.

"You know," said Beattie, "in the past, all information was doled out top-down. These days people look for ideas anywhere they can get them—technology, networking, informal meetings, and the like. Some of the greatest advances happen when people are bold enough to speak their truth and listen to others speak theirs—which is why I commend you on having your chat with Wayne. Great things can come from this, Dave."

"We'll see about that."

"To Primo II," said Beattie, raising her cup.

Dave clinked his cup against hers and they drank in unison.

CHAPTER 9

A Bit of a Breakthrough

After a brief but encouraging conversation with Dee before he left for work, Dave was feeling optimistic. But soon after reaching his office, he encountered turbulence. Lisa Virani called to ask him to intervene in a dispute the production department—her group—was having with research and development—Wayne's group—in the R&D conference room.

Dave entered the room to find a standoff: Wayne and his team, including Steve and Sarah, were sitting on one side of the table; Lisa and her group were sitting on the other. Lisa was directing some pointed questions at Wayne.

"I'm still not understanding, Wayne, why you can't release the Light Speed program to us. This is our chance to get Primo II off on the right foot. My understanding is that testing was finalized weeks ago and—"

"That's not the point, Lisa," Wayne interrupted.

The others fidgeted and averted their eyes, clearly uncomfortable with the heated exchange.

This is a classic example of how Cobalt desperately needs communication practices that allow people to feel free to say what's on their mind, Dave thought.

Hoping to prevent an all-out departmental war, Dave cleared his throat and said, "What seems to be the problem here? Lisa, what's Light Speed?"

"It's this amazing new workflow template Wayne's team has created—"

"Yes, our work *is* amazing, Lisa. That's the first sensible thing you've said this morning," interjected Wayne.

"But he won't share it with my team," Lisa continued. "The pilot test showed that it cuts production time by at least 8 percent, and it can cut production costs by up to 20 percent. I have every confidence that we can bring Primo II in on budget—or maybe even under—if we manage the project with Light Speed from the outset."

"And *I* don't feel it's ready for release," said Wayne flatly.

An uncomfortable silence followed.

Surprising the others from Wayne's side of the table, Steve Frazier began to speak. "Wayne, it's true that we aren't quite finished with the final version of Light Speed, but we could release the beta version internally right now. There's nothing really stopping us from doing that."

Wayne shot Steve a disapproving glance.

Steve persisted. "At least I can't think of a reason we can't give Lisa the beta version. Can anyone else?" Steve looked at his R&D colleagues.

Dave was impressed. Less than a year out of college, Steve was already willing to talk openly to his boss—a silo buster in action!

Sarah smiled at Steve and said, "I think it's a great idea."

Wayne grunted. "All right, go ahead and send it to Lisa." He looked at his watch. "I've got to run." He stood up and walked out.

Both teams looked at each other in stunned silence.

"Okay! I guess this meeting is adjourned," said Lisa cheerfully. Everyone stood and started to leave, conversing in low tones.

Lisa walked out with Dave. "Thanks for helping. Wayne does this all the time. I feel like I have to beg him for anything that comes out of his department. I never get what I need from him without a fight. It wastes everyone's time!"

Dave did his best to remain neutral. "That may be true, Lisa, but look at your behavior at this meeting. You were willing to confront Wayne about this issue and that's good. I know how frustrating it is when someone's unwilling to share information."

"It's more than frustrating; it's maddening. With Wayne it's always a joke, like, 'I'll have to kill you if I tell you.'" Lisa's words gathered speed as her anger rose to the surface. "He holds back information until the last minute and then he's arrogant or sarcastic when he finally lets go of it. You saw how he behaved in there. He's a total power player."

"Let's not make it personal," said Dave.

"You're right—I'm sorry," said Lisa. Then a new thought made her smile. "On the bright side, now we get to use Light Speed on Primo II. The process is pretty slick."

"So is collaboration, when it happens. And today it started with you, Lisa. Speaking of collaboration, is there anyone else at Cobalt who could benefit from the Light Speed program?"

"Yes. Anyone who's involved in product development and production could benefit."

"Then why are we sitting on this information?" Dave asked, thinking out loud.

Lisa gave Dave a pointed look. *"Exactly."*

***

Dave called an impromptu meeting of the Primo II group later that afternoon. This time, the first page of the flip chart described the details of the Hands domain.

> • The Hands are **what you do:** your actions and behavior during collaboration
> • **Open communication** is vital to collaboration

To Dave's surprise, Wayne showed up. Dave spent the first fifteen minutes of the meeting making sure everyone was clear on next steps for the project.

"Now I want to spend a few minutes talking about the Hands domain—what you do during collaboration. Clear communication is critical to any collaborative effort. So from here on, we're going to focus on sharing information—the more, the better. Be spontaneous if you want to. Network. Talk among yourselves! And don't be afraid to speak your truth. I want to encourage you to debate ideas. What's not okay is to sit on them, especially the brilliant ones. Right, Wayne?" Dave said with a smile.

"If you insist," Wayne said good-naturedly.

Dave continued. "The more we practice sharing what we know and what we've learned, the smarter we'll all be—and that makes for a stronger project. From here on out, our goal as we work toward the completion of Primo II will be to think with one mind. That means we need to knock down barriers to sharing and build new ways for people to access information faster than ever before. Any ideas on how we can do that?"

A hand went up to Dave's left and he called on Rachel Huang, one of Lisa's bright young colleagues in the production department.

"If we all had the same level of access to data and systems, that would be helpful," Rachel said.

"Great suggestion, Rachel. I'll talk to IT and the other department heads about that. We've got a lot of information posted on our company intranet, but we could definitely expand accessibility. Anyone else?"

Lisa said, "We need people from different departments to work together on projects more often. For example, what if our department borrowed Steve Frazier for a project? We could use his brains."

"That'll cost you," said Wayne.

"Fine," said Lisa. "Rachel, if it's okay with you, we'll send you over to R&D to help them on a project."

"Fine with me," agreed Rachel.

"I guess that wouldn't be a bad trade," said Wayne with a shrug.

"Rotating staff to share what they know with other departments is a terrific idea," said Dave. "Wayne, the people in your department are great. So are the people in your department, Lisa. And they'll be even greater together."

Encouraged, Dave spent the rest of the meeting listening to ideas about increasing the quality and quantity of information shared among the Primo II team members. As they talked, Dave realized the group was already talking openly, hardwiring the new principles of communication into the implementation of the project.

***

Back in his office, Dave captured his notes about collaborative communication:

Issues Around the HANDS Domain:

Open Communication
Problems:
- Leaders withheld information
- Leaders withheld team members from project
- Networking was discouraged
- Business plans were not communicated on a regular basis

Solutions:
- Increase information sharing
- Create opportunities for cross-functional teaming
- Encourage networking and spontaneous interaction
- Use technology to make business plans more widely available and readily accessible

---

As Dave was finishing up, Sarah appeared at his office doorway and gave a quick knock. Dave looked up.

"How's Dee?" she asked.

"She's home and doing fine. Thanks for asking," he said with a smile.

"Did everything go smoothly?"

"Yes, and it was amazing—she was able to go home only two hours after the biopsy."

"When do you get the results?"

"Hopefully by Friday," Dave said as his heart skipped a beat. He did his best to switch gears. "I thought it was a great meeting today," he said.

"I appreciate everything you're doing to drag this place into the twenty-first century," said Sarah. "Apart from being a smart way to work, collaborating is a lot more fun."

"I think so, too. People like you, Lisa, and Steve are showing everybody how it's done."

***

After experiencing Beattie's bland cooking, Dave decided it was time to spice things up a bit, so he brought home Thai takeout. He was so happy to see Dee up and around that he catered to her every need—which seemed to be irritating her a little.

"Dave, you're hovering," she said. "I know you mean well, honey, but give me a little space."

He laughed at himself and promised to back off.

As she sampled the green curry with chicken, Dee asked Dave if he'd made any progress with Primo II. He brought her up to date on his meeting about talking openly as well as his sluggish progress with Wayne.

"For as much of a pain as Wayne is, he's indispensable," Dave concluded. "He told me point blank he would need a monetary incentive to stay on the Primo II project. I really need to get him on my side."

"Do you know what to offer him?" Dee asked.

"No idea. That's why I need HR's help. Or any ideas *you* might have, Ms. HR Executive," he said with a smile.

"I wonder if Cobalt could make collaboration an organizational incentive."

"Wouldn't that be expensive?"

"Not necessarily. Incentives don't have to be about money. You can make collaboration an organizational competency or an explicit value."

"I've been thinking we could make collaborative behavior one of the criteria necessary for promotion."

"That's a good incentive," said Dee. "Maybe you could also establish a 'Collaborator of the Year' award."

"I like that idea," said Dave.

Beattie smiled and said, "That's my smart sister for you. She does her best thinking when she's high on painkillers."

Dee elbowed Beattie sharply in the ribs. Suddenly they were thirty years younger and back home in London.

As Dave watched the sisters laughing together, he remembered meeting the two of them at the London School of Economics—his first trip abroad. The Anderson girls had taken an instant liking to him and he'd become part of the family. He had liked them both, but it was Dee's red hair, quick wit, and gentle heart that had won him over.

Suddenly, Dave's stomach fluttered as fear about the pathology results crept into his mind. His heart ached for her, but unlike thirty years ago, it wasn't in a good way.

CHAPTER 10

Empower Yourself and Others

Sitting in Dr. Veronica Scott's office, Dave held Dee's hand and hoped she didn't feel him flinch as Dr. Scott delivered the news.

"Unfortunately, the results of the biopsy were positive—we did find a malignancy," she said. Dave heard Dee gasp softly. The doctor quickly continued.

"The good news is that because of your regular breast checks, we've detected the cancer at a very early stage. The lymph nodes we removed were clear, which is what we were hoping for. What this means for you is that a lumpectomy and a few radiation treatments should be all that's needed."

Dave gently squeezed his wife's hand and tried to look confident as the doctor discussed Dee's options. Remaining calm, Dee asked a few sensible questions in a steady voice. *She's dealing with this better than I am,* Dave thought.

The doctor recommended that Dee speak with the nurse specialist and mentioned there was also counseling service available.

"How soon will I be able to I have the surgery, Dr. Scott?"

"You have plenty of time to get a second opinion and do your own research before making a decision, but if you're ready to move forward with the lumpectomy, we could schedule surgery as soon as Thursday of next week. We found an opening on the calendar when the group was discussing your case yesterday afternoon."

"The group?" Dave asked.

Dr. Scott nodded. "Our medical group uses a collaborative approach to patient care, so there's a lot of interdisciplinary talent and communication involved in each patient's treatment."

"That sounds like a great system," said Dave.

"I can assure you that you'll get the best care possible," Dr. Scott continued, her eyes on Dee. "Our surgeons, nurses, and other specialists have a tremendous amount of combined experience and knowledge. We've designed our health care delivery system in a way so that every member of the team brings all of their insight and skills to each patient's treatment."

"I'd like to deal with this right away," said Dee with a determined expression. "I've done my research. I'm ready."

"All right, we'll get the paperwork started," Dr. Scott said. "You'll be meeting with the surgery team between now and Thursday so that you'll have a complete picture of what to expect."

Dave and Dee stood to go. Dave hadn't let go of Dee's hand—nor had she let go of his—through the entire appointment.

***

Beattie decided to extend her stay in order to take Dee to her pre-op appointments and support both Dave and Dee through the surgery. Over the next several days she lightened the mood around the house with her dry British humor. They all did their best to stay cheerful, count their blessings, and cope with this new reality.

During one of their now-customary early morning coffee and tea sessions, Beattie took a break from her email to chat with Dave.

"These past few days as I've taken Dee to her appointments, I've seen for myself what your doctor told you about how her surgical team collaborates. They discuss issues and explore alternative ideas and solutions together until they come to a mutual decision."

"That's right," said Dave. "Dr. Scott told us they use a multidisciplinary approach where the best and brightest from every department bring their talents to the table."

"Ah," said Beattie. "They practice the second key part of the Hands domain—empowerment.

The hospital has created an environment that empowers everyone to share knowledge. It makes me feel more confident than ever about Dee having her surgery there."

Dave grabbed his notepad and wrote *Empowerment* on a clean page. "Tell me more about how empowerment fits into collaboration so that I can share it with the group."

"The first thing you need to stress is that empowerment, like collaboration, begins at the *individual* level," said Beattie.

"How is that?" asked Dave.

"In a culture of collaboration, individual contributors see themselves as self leaders. Leaders empower these individuals by building trust and coaching competence in their job roles and networking skills. And individuals also empower and inspire each other when they share ideas and deliver on their allotted tasks or goals."

"I get it. Empowered people feel more trusted and competent, and therefore feel more of an individual responsibility to contribute—like they are a bigger part of the organization. And I like the idea of empowering each other."

"Exactly. At Blenheim, after we started emphasizing the power of love rather than the love of power, we discovered that when knowledge is shared, so are power and influence, decision making, and accountability. Everyone takes responsibility for achieving the goals. And when power is distributed, everyone relies less on formal position power and more on expertise and networks."

"That sounds a lot like when Dr. Scott said that Dee would be getting the best care possible, because so many specialists were contributing to her treatment. It's completely different from what I remember when I had hernia surgery many years ago. I had a doctor who seemed to command every aspect of the operation. Now that I remember back, I had some trouble getting information and there was a mix-up about my medication."

"I'm glad you lived through it," said Beattie with a smile.

"Me, too." Dave smiled back. "So what about leaders like Wayne and some of the other old school micromanagers? Doesn't the idea of people empowering each other feel like a threat to their way of leading?"

"It absolutely can. Remember when we were talking about implementation, when direct reports become responsible and empowered self leaders? That's when the leader's job switches from a command-and-control directing role to a more responsive coaching role. It's a tough transition for some leaders. It takes time to get everyone on board. The good news is that once leaders embrace the role of coach, they realize the weight of leadership is now balanced between themselves and their direct reports. Keep in mind that a collaborative leader must still set work direction, resolve conflict, and remove obstacles. But they are there to coach and sponsor collaborative work rather than oversee it. They set their egos aside and let the team deliver."

Dave looked at his watch. "I've got to get going, but as usual, thanks for the coaching." He glanced over his notes. "Oh—I do have one last question."

"Okay," said Beattie.

"We've covered utilizing differences and creating an environment of safety and trust under the Heart domain, creating a clear purpose, values, and goals under the Head domain, and open communication and empowerment under the Hands domain. Which of these do you feel is the most important key to collaboration?"

"It's rather like collaboration itself," said Beattie. "They're all important, because they're interdependent. You can't just do a bit of one and some of the other."

"So you have to have all the switches turned on all the time, so to speak?"

"Yes, but depending on where you are on any given project, some will be amplified. For example, the first thing you do to ensure everyone is aligned will be to work together to establish the purpose, values, and goals. Next, you'll want to create a trusting atmosphere so that people feel secure about surfacing ideas and concerns. And so on."

"Makes sense to me," said Dave as he stood to go. "The big question is: Will it make sense to my CEO?"

CHAPTER 11

Collaboration at Work: A Real World Example

Early Thursday morning, Dave sat with Dee in the back seat of the car as Beattie taxied them to the hospital. Holding Dee's hand, he prayed that the surgery would go smoothly and that she would heal according to schedule.

Dee looked over at him. "Sweetheart, please wipe that worried look off your face. I'm going to be fine. I'm visualizing that nasty cancer leaving my body today and never coming back."

"That's a fantastic idea. I'll think about that, too." He smiled. "Aren't I the one who's supposed to be comforting you?"

Beattie laughed as she looked in the rearview mirror at her passengers. "Don't be fooled by Dee's delicate exterior, Dave," she said. "Under that soft skin is a woman of steel. Surely you know that by now."

Once they got to the hospital, Beattie and Dave watched as Margery, the concierge, again guided Dee through the check-in process. As they approached the pre-op unit, Margery turned to Beattie and said, "Unfortunately, only

Mr. Oakman is allowed to accompany his wife from here."

With that, Beattie said, "You've got this, sis. I love you." She hugged Dee.

In the pre-op area, Dee met with what Dave called her 'collaborative team.' She was seen by her oncologist, a phlebotomist, an anesthesiologist, and a nurse specialist. Dave was impressed by the way these people all handled their responsibilities. After introducing themselves, they each checked Dee's chart for information they needed to know and then updated the chart for the benefit of their colleagues.

"You really do work collaboratively at this hospital, don't you?" Dave said to the nurse specialist.

"Absolutely," she said. "If we didn't, we'd put patients at risk—and the welfare of the patient is our number one value."

Dave made a mental note to share this interaction with his project group.

The nurse specialist oversaw Dee's transfer to the surgical suite. Dave embraced his wife as she lay on the gurney.

"I love you, Dee. Beattie and I will be here when you come around, okay?"

"Okay, honey. It will be a great feeling to wake up on the other side of this procedure," said Dee optimistically.

Dave kissed her and then watched as orderlies rolled the gurney down the hall and through the double doors to surgery. He knew she was in the hands of experts.

Needing some alone time, Dave bought a magazine at the gift shop and found what he thought would be a quiet place to read and gather his thoughts.

He soon realized he wasn't alone, however, as he began to notice medical staff members coming and going through a nearby open doorway. While he couldn't make out every word, Dave could tell they were discussing diagnoses, prognoses, and action plans. He realized he was overhearing a culture of collaboration in action. Every case was discussed as a unique and complex situation. There were even occasional disagreements that seemed to resolve after some discussion. At one point he heard the phrase "Let's try a new approach" and observed as a variety of medical personnel arrived to share their expertise.

An older man with a stethoscope draped around his neck walked out of the doorway, saw Dave, and approached him.

At that very moment, Dave noticed a sign on the wall that read *Staff Only*.

"I'm Dr. Maalouf. May I help you?" the man said, extending his hand.

"Dave Oakman," said Dave, standing up and shaking the doctor's hand. "I'm sorry—I just realized I'm trespassing."

"No worries," said the doctor with a smile. "I will need to ask you to move, though. You're in the Clinical Decisions Unit and we need to be sure patient information is kept confidential."

"Of course," said Dave. "I'll head back to the family waiting area. My wife is in surgery."

"I'm going that direction, too. I'll join you."

As they began walking Dave said, "I'm very impressed by how patient centered this hospital is."

"That's by design," said Dr. Maalouf. "The staff here works together in a very conscientious way to get people well and back home as soon as possible."

"I couldn't help but notice that you bring a lot of specialists into the decision making process, including nurses and younger doctors," said Dave.

"Of course. Without our multidisciplinary team, we'd be dealing with insufficient data. Our residents have a lot of innovative ideas, and our nurses often have the most reliable patient information. We all need to keep learning and building our experience. It's a no-brainer, really. We want to treat each patient in the most effective and efficient manner possible. Sometimes getting input from several specialists takes extra time and effort, but that's what keeps our success rate high."

"Every time I am here, I'm more impressed with the way things are done. It's comforting to know my wife is getting the best care possible," said Dave.

When they reached the waiting area, they said goodbye and Dr. Maalouf headed for the elevator. Dave could see Beattie reading her tablet as he approached her. She was holding a bouquet of flowers.

"For me?" Dave joked.

Beattie looked up and smiled. "Of course not, you numpty—they're for my sister!"

Dave sat down and suddenly felt uneasy. "Have you heard anything yet?"

"No, but then it hasn't been that long. At this point I suppose things are well underway."

Dave closed his eyes, said a quick prayer, and then remembered what Dee had said in the car. He pictured the cancer leaving her body forever. He was surprised at the amount of comfort that small activity gave him.

He pulled his laptop out of his shoulder bag and started to work while Beattie continued reading. Both frequently glanced at the time. After another hour—which included a quick trip to the coffee stand—Dave hit the Save button and looked expectantly around the room. He was having trouble concentrating on work.

Just then, as if he had willed it, Margery came around the corner.

"Excuse me, Mr. Oakman?"

"Yes," Dave said, feeling a tremor in his gut. Beattie looked up.

"The surgery went very well, as expected. Dr. Scott wanted me to tell you she was able to remove the mass with clear margins all around. Your wife is fine and is now in recovery. I'll let you know when we have her room ready and you can wait there for her. It shouldn't be too long."

Beattie squeezed Dave's hand and they both let out sighs of relief.

Hearing this news took Dave's anxiety down several notches. He thanked Margery and then said, "You know, I had never heard of a hospital with a concierge before coming here."

Margery smiled. "I hadn't either, until I got this job. It's amazing, isn't it? I worked as a flight attendant for many years and wanted to cut down on my travel, so when I saw a posting for this position I jumped at it. It was a perfect fit for my background. I'm one of six concierges here."

After Margery left, Dave turned to Beattie and said, "I meant to tell you, when I was walking around, I accidentally ended up in a staff area and got to overhear collaboration in action. There was a gathering of specialists from different departments and they were having discussions and making treatment decisions together. I even heard a couple of disagreements but they were quickly worked out. There sure don't seem to be many silos around here."

"I'm certainly impressed. If I have any medical problems, you may see me back here!"

Knowing Dee was safely in recovery, Dave was finally able to get his head back into his work and do a final polish on his report. A short time later he turned to Beattie and said, "There. I've finished."

"Finished what?" asked Beattie, looking up from her tablet.

"A couple of things, actually. First, my notes on how we can empower each other at Cobalt." Dave brought up the document on his laptop and showed it to Beattie:

Issues Around the HANDS Domain:

Empowerment
Problems:
- Leaders placed blame instead of allowing space for mistakes and learning
- Leaders saw control as power, and were reluctant to give it up
- Leaders felt they were not in control if they were not micromanaging
- Micromanagement by leaders led to mistrust by direct reports
- People who don't trust leaders can't become empowered self leaders

Solutions:
- To empower individual contributors, leaders coach for competence and build trust
- Leaders and direct reports agree when to check in and review work progress
- Leaders coach direct reports in networking skills

> • Power is distributed between leaders and the people in their work unit

"That's excellent," said Beattie. What else did you finish?"

"The full and final Primo report for Jim. It includes all of my notes about problems and solutions, as well as the list of Primo's specific flaws. It actually turned into a kind of justification for implementing collaboration—not only within the Primo II project, but throughout the company as well."

Beattie smiled. "May I read it?"

"Of course," Dave said, "but not until I show you what I discovered."

"Please do," said Beattie lightheartedly. "It's fun to see the things your ingenious mind comes up with."

"So I've been trying to figure out an easy way for everyone at Cobalt to remember the keys to a collaborative culture. That way, when we begin applying it, it has the best chance of catching on. I decided an acronym would be perfect. So I started rephrasing the points about listening to different perspectives, creating safety and trust, coming up with a purpose, values, and goals, communicating openly, and empowering everyone, and look what happened." He turned his laptop so Beattie could see the model he had created.

Heart: Who you are as a collaborative leader— your character and intentions	➡ **U**tilize differences ➡ **N**urture safety and trust
Head: What you know—your beliefs and attitudes about collaboration	➡ **I**nvolve others in crafting a clear purpose, values, and goals
Hands: What you do—your actions and behavior during collaboration	➡ **T**alk openly ➡ **E**mpower yourself and others

Beattie gasped. "You truly *are* brilliant!"

Dave smiled. "Each letter of the word *UNITE* represents an approach necessary for a collaborative culture. On a project like Primo II, focusing on the UNITE model can remind everyone how to work together in a collaborative way."

"So now you can say to effectively collaborate, everyone needs to UNITE on projects."

"Exactly! I even put this model in my report for Jim. Here it comes—let me know what you think." Dave clicked Send and emailed the full report to Beattie so she could read it on her tablet.

A few minutes later Beattie looked up at Dave. "This sums it up nicely. I do have a few pointers, though." She suggested that Dave include an assessment that could be used at the individual, team, and organizational levels, as well as a listing of specific actions Cobalt could take to increase collaboration.

"I'd be happy to help you with those," she said.

Margery soon returned to escort them to Dee's room.

Soon afterward, Dave and Beattie were waiting with flowers and balloons as a hospital worker rolled Dee's bed into her room. Still groggy from the anesthetic, her emerald eyes were fluttering as she tried to stay awake.

Dave bent over her bed and kissed her cheek. "You look as beautiful as ever," he said.

"You're a trouper, sis," added Beattie.

A pained smile crossed Dee's lips. Disoriented, she murmured something about the Tower of London.

"What's that, honey?" Dave asked, but she was once again asleep.

CHAPTER 12

Getting Things Done

Dave and Beattie stopped at the hospital on Friday morning to visit with Dee. Barring any unexpected complications, she was scheduled for release later that afternoon. With Dee sore but in good spirits and Beattie planning to stay with her for the day, Dave returned to work.

The Primo II group filed into the conference room at 10:30. Dave noticed Wayne was absent but started the meeting on time by adding the second element of the Hands domain, which he had written on the flip chart:

> The hands are **what you do:** your actions and behavior during collaboration
> **Open communication** is vital to collaboration and leads to **empowerment**—of yourself and others

"I hope you non-managers in the room are already beginning to see yourselves as important contributors. Let me see a show of hands if you are," asked Dave.

More than half the hands in the room went up.

"Good! I'm going to expand on that idea. Under the Hands domain of collaboration, communicating openly goes hand in hand—pun intended—with empowerment. As trust and information sharing become the norm, first within our Primo II project group and ultimately within Cobalt as a whole, individual contributors will become more and more competent in their roles. Leaders will see and encourage this competence, creating empowered self leaders. When these individuals work together, sharing ideas and cheering each other on, they automatically empower each other to reach their goals. Empowered people, working together, create a remarkable synergy where the group as a whole is far greater than the sum of its parts. Everyone benefits in this scenario."

Anthony raised his hand and Dave called his name.

"I think a lot of us would love that kind of environment. I know it would make me feel like I was contributing to the company's success—like it was my success, too. But what if a manager doesn't want to give up control? What if they don't want to empower their direct reports?"

Dave spoke carefully. "It's to the leader's significant advantage to share information, encourage networking, and sponsor collaborative work rather than commanding and controlling people. Leaders still need to set the vision and direction, settle differences, and coach their direct reports—but the pressure on them is greatly reduced because their relationships with people will feel much more like partnerships. Sometimes it's not a quick or easy transition, but I intend to offer my support to all of the managers involved in Primo II, to make things as smooth as possible."

Dave then described the way his wife's surgical team had collaborated before and during her surgery.

"That's the way I'd like to see us all work together on this project," Dave said. "Everyone I encountered was a high achieving, empowered contributor. It seemed to me that they liked their jobs and were proud of their workplace."

Dave regretted Wayne's absence. He wanted him to hear about this real world example of collaboration and service, in the hope that the message would get through.

The group seemed genuinely interested in Dave's story. Several people expressed their best wishes for Dee's recovery, which lifted his spirits. He also shared the UNITE acronym as an easy way to remember the Heart, Head, and Hands components necessary for effective collaboration.

Twenty minutes into the meeting, when the group was in the middle of a discussion about the problems that had drained the profit out of the first Primo project, Wayne walked in.

"Wayne, I'm glad you're here," said Dave. "We're talking right now about some of the reasons we took a loss on Primo and how we can keep it from happening again. I'd like to have your input."

"Input, huh? Like what?"

Everyone was silent. Eyes darted from Dave to Wayne and back again.

"Well, you're the specialist in this area. I was hoping you could bring some technical expertise to the table," said Dave. He briefly described a glitch in a software program used for Primo that had been found to be one of the sources of the cost overrun.

Wayne sat back in silence, arms crossed over his chest.

The two men stared at one another across the table. Just as Dave was beginning to feel like a contestant in a game of chicken, Steve Frazier broke the silence and suggested a specific kind of fix to solve the problem.

"That won't work," Wayne said, shooting down the idea before Steve had even finished speaking.

He didn't even think before responding to Steve's suggestion, thought Dave. He recognized Wayne's reaction as an automatic control response. Wayne needed to be in charge and, more important, to be *seen as* being in charge. New ideas were *his* job, not the job of his direct reports. *How can I help change this attitude? I have to remember—patience and persistence!*

The young engineer didn't back down. "Actually, I think with some tweaks and a partial rewrite of the code, I could get the program to perform in a way that would alleviate the problem."

Dave was delighted to see Steve in silo-busting mode again, taking the initiative to be heard. Wayne had a different reaction. His face reddened and a vein appeared in his forehead. He clearly was irritated at Steve's self-assuredness.

"What about the other projects you're working on? Do you have time for this?" Wayne blustered.

"I don't have to deliver on Omen for eight weeks. And Elysium is fairly elastic in terms of time, too. I can do this, Wayne." Steve's enthusiasm burned brightly in his eyes.

Dave threw Steve a lifeline. "Why don't you expand on your idea a little more," he said.

That was all the encouragement Steve needed. He outlined his general plan, clearly up for the challenge. For the first time there were smiles around the room. Even Wayne relaxed, seeming to enjoy the reflected glory.

As Steve talked, Dave observed this new silo buster closely. It was clear Steve was not only smart but also willing to share what he knew. In the few months he had worked at Cobalt, he hadn't succumbed to Wayne's bulldozer temperament. Dave realized that Steve was part of the new generation that loved the challenge of solving complex problems, bringing new ideas to life, and sharing them with others. It was evident from his behavior that he believed knowledge belonged to everyone—and collaboration was everyone's responsibility, starting with him.

Steve turned to Wayne, confident and calm. "So what do you think, Wayne? Can I go ahead and help them with this?"

Dave held his breath as Wayne pondered the question.

"All right," Wayne said at last. "I'll allow it. As long as your other work doesn't suffer."

Dave felt a surge of goodwill toward Wayne. He was obviously struggling to be collaborative and at the same time remain in control—or at least appear to remain in control. *This could be the beginning of Wayne's turnaround,* Dave thought.

"That's great—thanks, Wayne," said Dave. "If you need additional resources while Steve works on this, let me know and I'll do what I can to get them to you. I think we all know what a strategic piece of business Primo II is."

The meeting ended and the group members gathered up their things and began to leave the room, chatting amiably. As Steve headed toward the door, Dave walked up and shook his hand.

"Steve, I'm really impressed with the way you conducted yourself at this meeting. You proved that to make collaboration work, individuals need to step up and make the decision to work together with others for the greater good. I can see that you understand collaboration begins with you."

"Thanks, Dave," said Steve, smiling as he turned and left the room.

Wayne hung back. When the last of the Primo II group had cleared out, he walked up to Dave and stood inches from his face. "Listen, buddy," he hissed, "don't think I don't know what you're doing here."

"I don't appreciate your tone, Wayne. The only thing I'm doing here is trying to get everyone to work together on a very complex project for the good of the company—and all of us."

Wayne stepped back but didn't back down. "Don't you ever commandeer my people like that again. We've worked together a long time, Dave. I've never interfered with your department. I even congratulated you when you got promoted! I don't think I deserve to be treated the way you just treated me."

Dave was puzzled by Wayne's outburst. He hadn't directly asked Steve to help—Steve volunteered and Wayne agreed. Remembering Beattie's good advice, Dave didn't take Wayne's challenge personally but he did take it seriously. "What's the real issue here, Wayne?"

"The issue, Dave," Wayne said in a rising voice, "is that I was put in a difficult position and you were in charge. Steve works for me, and that means *I* tell him what to work on, this group doesn't. And *he* doesn't get to decide, either. That protocol was just violated. All these years working alongside each other, and now you decide to tread on my toes."

Beattie's words rang in Dave's ears: *Where there is conflict, there is creativity. Don't make it personal. Stay on the issue.*

"Wayne, can't you spare Steve?"

Wayne shrugged. "I suppose I can spare him. He's a good guy and he always gets his work done."

"So what's the problem?"

"The problem is that this group, under your leadership, doesn't respect that I get to say what Steve works on, and when."

"Okay. I get that you're upset because you feel I encroached on your territory, that Steve is your employee and you call the shots with his schedule." Dave was using classic active listening skills so Wayne would know his concerns were being heard. Dave knew he had to win this one—and he wanted to do it in a fair way, without getting angry.

"Damn right I call the shots," Wayne grumbled.

"I want to remind you, though, that you were the one just now who gave Steve permission to go ahead."

"Yeah, but only because I was backed into a corner."

Dave nodded. "I can see how it would feel that way." He took a deep breath. "Look—can I be straight with you?"

Wayne looked puzzled. "Sure."

Dave picked up a copy of the report he was finishing for Jim and handed it to Wayne.

"Jim asked—actually, he demanded—that I report on what went wrong with Primo. Here's the final draft of my report—it's all but finished and I'll be turning it in to Jim tomorrow. I'm not sure whether you actually read the first draft I gave you last week, but I want to you to read this one."

Wayne grumbled something Dave couldn't understand.

Not backing off, Dave continued. "I found a lot of issues, but I'll give you the short version: We have to change the way we do business around here. Wayne, you're one of the best and brightest people this company has. But like me, you learned your management style from business people who lived in a different world. Technology hasn't just changed the way we communicate; it's changed the way people problem solve, innovate, and act."

With a nod of his head, Wayne begrudgingly agreed.

"The caste system is dead, and collaboration is the way things are done. As leaders, we have to model collaborative behavior—especially if we want to keep our younger talent and stay ahead of the competition."

Wayne looked at the report in his hand. "So you really think the solution to our profit shortfall is collaboration?"

Dave nodded. "You told me a while ago that money is your motivator, and I'm pretty sure you're not the only manager who feels that way. So I'm working on an incentive program for managers who collaborate. If you help us on Primo II, I'll make sure you're first in line. And if we get it right this time, our share price will increase—and our bonuses will follow."

"Okay, I'll read your report," Wayne said.

"Good," said Dave. "By the way, you did an outstanding job recruiting Steve. He has fresh ideas and he's not afraid to share them. You've always had a great eye for talent, but in his case you've outdone yourself." Dave meant every word of it.

"Thanks. Steve's a good guy." For the first time, Wayne's face relaxed. "By the way, how is Dee? I heard she has cancer."

Dave was surprised—and touched—at the question. In all the years they'd worked at Cobalt together, the only personal information Wayne and Dave had ever exchanged was golf scores.

"Thanks for asking. She had surgery yesterday and it went well. Her prognosis is good. I'm actually bringing her home later this afternoon," Dave said.

"That's great to hear," said Wayne with a pleasant smile.

***

That night at home, Dave logged off his laptop just after midnight. Dee had come home feeling as well as could be expected and had fallen asleep soon afterward. The nurse specialist had told Dave and Beattie that Dee would be tired and sore for a few days and would probably need their help.

Dave was relieved to have his concerns about Dee's surgery behind him. He felt positive about his conversation with Wayne and was also feeling good about his progress on the final draft of the Primo report for Jim. He had finished the assessments and action plan Beattie had suggested and had also added a few new ideas to the section on problems and solutions. Leaving his study, he noticed the kitchen light was still on. He decided to have a nightcap.

Dave poured a small brandy before realizing Beattie was sitting at the kitchen table, reading.

"Can I pour you a brandy?" he asked.

"Sure, why not?" Beattie put her tablet aside and raised the glass Dave handed to her. "To our recovering patient," she said. "She came through with flying colors."

"Thank God for that," said Dave.

"Now we need to force her to take it easy for a while," said Beattie with a smile.

"I'm going to wait on her, hand and foot, all weekend," said Dave. "She's going to get really annoyed with me, and I don't care."

They sipped their drinks and fell into a long communal silence.

"As much as I've loved being here with you and Dee, it will be good to be back in my own bed by the end of the week," said Beattie wistfully.

"Your visit couldn't have been timed any better, Beattie. I honestly don't know what we would have done without you." Dave felt a catch in his throat and decided to stop there.

"By the time I leave, my wonderful sister will be well on the road to 100 percent—and I can tell you are back in the swing of things at Cobalt."

"Thanks mostly to you, Ms. Anderson," said Dave. Beattie looked down at her glass and smiled.

Dave continued. "I've finished revising the report along the lines you suggested. I think it's really, finally, finished,"

"Got the assessment in there?" Beattie asked.

"Yep. I also went ahead and told Jim about the clear purpose, values, and goals we've already established for Primo II. I wanted him to see we were already acting on what I was learning."

"It must be a relief to be done with the thing."

"You have no idea." Dave took a sip of brandy. "Actually, you probably do!" he exclaimed, and they both laughed. "Anyway, I'm not waiting until Monday—I'm going to email it to Jim in the morning."

***

"So what's the latest with your big report?" asked Dee. She was sitting up in bed and had just finished a light breakfast Dave had prepared and brought to her on a tray.

"I was hoping you'd ask," said Dave with a smile as he handed her the report. They had always shared the highs and lows of their workdays, helping one another through various scenarios through the years. He knew her asking about the report was a positive sign that she was starting to recover.

"I finished it last night and emailed it to Jim first thing this morning. You don't have to read it until you feel up to it. I don't want you wearing yourself out. You need to rest."

"I promise I'll only read it if I'm dying of boredom," said Dee with a smirk.

"You're not going to die of anything, especially my work. Jim seems to have a better attitude toward truth telling lately—which is a good thing, because I told a *lot* of truth in that report. I wonder what he will think."

CHAPTER 13

A Turnaround—and a Plan

Monday morning, Dave got a call from Trish Ward, Jim's assistant.

"Jim wants to see you in his office this morning. Can you meet with him at ten?"

"Sure," said Dave, surprising himself with his sense of confidence.

Dave had been sending Jim bits and pieces of the Primo report as he went along but hadn't received any feedback. Now that Jim had the full report, Dave wasn't sure exactly what to expect as he walked into Jim's office.

Jim was standing at his window. He turned to Dave and waved a hand toward one of the chairs around his mahogany conference table.

"Have a seat," Jim said.

Dave couldn't read his mood. Jim sat at the table next to him and looked him in the eye.

"Good report, Dave," he said with a sudden smile.

Even with his higher level of confidence, a wave of relief flowed through Dave's body. "I'm glad you think so. I thought I might have stated a few things too candidly."

"What I've learned lately is that candor is precisely what we need more of around here. As I read this report I was reminded of my late father, who was an admiral in the U.S. Navy. He always told me, 'If you don't hear complaining from the people around you, you'd better watch your behind, because you're going over the side.' I need to know what the problems are around here before there's mutiny."

"I don't think things are that bad, Jim. But I'm glad you're open to hearing new ideas. I was encouraged when you talked about reevaluating your leadership style. I've been doing the same. I think we can all learn from analyzing what went wrong with the Primo project."

"I agree," said Jim. "In terms of the report, I'm really intrigued by your three domains of collaboration—the Heart, the Head, and the Hands—and also the UNITE acronym you came up with. Almost every page of this report made me think about my own leadership behavior. Now more than ever, I get it. Yes, Cobalt needs work, but I have to make some changes at a personal level, too. In both areas, I have to trust more—no more second-guessing every decision that's made by someone other than me. And I have to create a safe environment. I have a bad habit of keeping people worried about their jobs, even if I don't threaten them outright."

Hearing that, Dave breathed even easier.

"That said," Jim continued, "we need to talk about Wayne. Look, Dave, I know your report doesn't call anyone out by name, but it's clear that Wayne is a major problem. I've worked with him enough to know that his attitude is lousy, much like mine has been in the past. If we're really going to build a collaborative culture around here, give me one good reason why we should keep Wayne."

"Because getting rid of Wayne would create more problems than it would solve," Dave answered. "He's certainly not the only manager here who has a territorial approach. If we start firing people, it will undermine the very safety and trust we need to start cultivating. Besides, Wayne needs an opportunity to learn the same way we're learning during this process."

"You may have a point there."

"Wayne's not a bad guy, Jim, any more than you and I are."

"Tell my wife," Jim said with a weary smile. "Although because of the counseling we're getting, I think we're going to get through this and come out better on the other side."

"That's great news," said Dave with a smile.

"So you really believe Wayne can change?" Jim seemed unconvinced.

"I really believe Wayne wants to do the right thing," said Dave. "He probably learned his controlling style from somebody else who wanted to do the right thing. Who knows?

Maybe at one time it *was* the right thing. But it's just not viable in a twenty-first-century global economy."

"What about his focus on personal gain at the expense of company profit?" asked Jim. "That points to a character issue."

"Again, I have to say that may be a product of Cobalt's operating system. Our mantra has always been 'success at all costs'—or if not our mantra, it's certainly been our culture. Given that environment, over the years Wayne has delivered what the company has asked of him. He may be an entirely different person at home. Maybe he thinks we don't want nice guys here at Cobalt."

"Maybe," admitted Jim.

"Think of it this way: when Wayne expresses his thoughts so bluntly, we could see it as an opportunity to address concerns others feel but nobody else has the guts to talk openly about. Maybe if we didn't have Wayne, we'd have to *invent* him. We need someone who's bold enough to bring up important issues we never think about, like tying compensation to collaborative leadership."

Jim nodded. "Now there's an idea."

Dave became more animated as he continued. "Jim, I think we can instill in everyone the idea that collaboration begins with you—with me—with each one of us. Everyone at Cobalt, not just managers, needs to consider who they are, what they believe, and what they can accomplish when they collaborate. When that happens, it will start changing the way people feel about collaboration—like it did for you when we started talking about what went wrong with Primo. Then interdepartmental dynamics will change and so will Cobalt's whole self-serving, siloed culture. And it'll be a change not just for the common good, but for the *greater* good of the company."

"Okay, first things first," said Jim as he rose from the table. "Let's get Primo II launched. Go ahead and use the project as a beta test for your collaboration approach. Set your sights on those four goals you and your group established—the company makes a nice profit, contributors feel valued, the client gives us a contract for Primo III, and the collaboration process works. After you and your group achieve success with Primo II—and I have confidence that you will—we'll have time to focus on implementing a collaborative culture throughout the company. And we'll do it together."

Dave stood up and saluted Jim. "Aye, aye, sir! You won't see any argument from me about that, and no talk of mutiny, sir!" They laughed and shook hands. Dave left Jim's office with a renewed drive to make Primo II the best example of collaboration Cobalt had ever seen.

CHAPTER 14

Six Months Later

With Dee's health rapidly returning to normal and Beattie back in the UK, Dave came home every night and shared the daily happenings on the Primo II project with his wife, best friend, and resident HR expert. He was amazed to see how quickly everyone on the project united together to create a collaborative culture. Sarah, Steve, Lisa, and everyone else got fired up—and their enthusiasm was contagious. The group's positive energy about the superior product they were creating together even changed Wayne into a willing contributor. Primo II ended up a win-win: not only did Cobalt make a significant profit, but the client loved the product and a new contract for Primo III became a reality.

***

Dave was energized as he headed to Jim's office for a one-on-one meeting to discuss plans for Primo III. He was ready to sink his teeth into the new project and already had names to suggest for potential new team members, along with ideas about what they could contribute.

He marveled as he recalled the anxiety he used to feel about meeting with Jim. They had a completely different relationship now—it felt like a partnership.

But after they greeted each other and sat down, Jim's expression stiffened. "Dave, I know you expected to talk about Primo III. But before we do, I need to let you know about a big change that's coming. It's been in the works for some time, but I couldn't tell you about it until now."

The old familiar feeling of dread gripped Dave by the throat. *Why haven't I heard about this big change? What have I done wrong now?* he thought.

"I want you to start thinking about who else can head up Primo III—because I'm pulling you off the project."

"What!" Dave blurted. He felt like he'd had the wind knocked out of him. "But why, Jim? Primo II was a huge success, both technically and financially. The project group came together as a unit and got the job done on time and under budget. The client loved the product and we got a new contract. I don't understand. Collaboration worked exactly as we thought it would!" He was running out of things to say. He felt like he was fighting for his job.

"Hold on, Dave," Jim held up his hand and smiled. "Listen to me. The reason I'm pulling you off Primo III is because a few weeks ago I recommended to our board of directors that we create a new position and that you should fill it: chief operating officer."

Cobalt's COO? It was the last thing Dave would have expected. Before he could open his mouth, Jim continued.

"You've had the respect of the leadership team for a long time and your peers hold you in high regard. You turned in a brilliant, forward-thinking report where you analyzed the results of the first Primo project and audaciously proposed sweeping changes to the way Cobalt does business. The overwhelming success of Primo II clinched it. The official announcement won't happen until after the board meets next week, but the decision has been made. It's a done deal, Dave. Congratulations."

Dave was stunned. "I'm honored, Jim."

"Your first order of business as COO will be to implement your model of collaboration companywide, as you laid it out for me. We're going to think of this as major surgery, Dave. No half measures. It won't be quick and it won't be easy, but as I said before, I'm going to give you my wholehearted support. You've opened my eyes to the fact that this company has been sick for quite a while. I believe creating a collaborative culture is how we're going to get healthy."

Jim picked up his phone and dialed a four-digit extension. "Jennifer, are you available to join Dave and me in my office? Okay, see you in a few."

"Jennifer Rosenberg in HR?" Dave asked.

Jim nodded.

"Before she gets here," said Dave, "let me clear up one thing. This is not *my* model. I learned it from my Brit sister-in-law."

"I appreciate your modesty," said Jim, "but *you* learned it and put it into action—and I believe you have what it takes to implement it throughout the organization."

There was a knock on the door. Jennifer appeared, slightly out of breath, and said, "I have to tell you, I practically sprinted over here. After I finished reading your report and recommendations, Dave, I stood up and pumped my fist in the air. I think I even said '*Yes!*' out loud. I've been trying to talk Jim into a culture change for the past two years! Cobalt needs a culture where—as you said in your report—people 'instinctively share what they know and work together with a clear purpose, guided by values, toward agreed-upon goals.' I actually memorized that line."

"What do you think of the UNITE acronym?" Dave asked.

"It really makes the Heart, Head, and Hands come alive," said Jennifer. "It's a great template for guiding the changes we need to make. I just need a little direction on the best way to start implementing it."

Jim broke in. "That's why I've brought you two together. I want you to put your heads together and mastermind this change. You both care deeply about the company and our people. I'm counting on you to engage and nurture our young talent so that they'll stay around and help lead this company into the future. At the same time, we need to bring our more seasoned people up to speed in a way that shows we care and respect their experience."

"This is going to take a while," said Jennifer.

"Most things worth doing take time," said Jim. "For now, plan your approach and let me know your ideas before the end of the month. The sooner we start, the sooner we can get this company back to being the industry leader it once was. Now, I know you both have a lot on your plates, so I'll let you get to it."

Jennifer was still smiling as she left the room. As Dave headed for the door, Jim called after him.

"Dave—any recommendations for the Primo III director job?" he asked.

Dave turned around. After a brief pause he said, "Yes. Wayne Lundgren."

"What?" Jim looked at Dave like he had suddenly sprouted horns.

"Wayne really came around during Primo II, Jim. Even when we disagreed, he just needed a bit of redirection to stay focused on the issues and he was fine. He brought a lot of expertise to the table and was more generous than ever before about sharing his department's talent for the good of the project."

"Hmm," said Jim.

Dave continued. "After doing some research on his own—and Wayne is a brilliant researcher—he told me he can finally see the value in busting the silos around here so we can all work more openly and collaboratively. He admitted that the Cobalt reward system had kept him focused more on his own department's results and made him slower to collaborate. But like you, Jim, he also said he now understands why it's important to listen to younger associates and see them as real contributors."

Now it was Jim's turn to be surprised. "Wow," he said.

"And this is even before anyone ties Wayne's compensation to collaboration," Dave said with a smile.

"Are you serious about recommending him to lead Primo III?"

"Serious as I've ever been," said Dave. "Wayne may be old school, but he's still one of the brightest minds in the company. I'm not saying all of his rough edges will be smoothed out overnight. But I'll be here to support him when he needs it. I think as long as we give him clear direction about Primo III's purpose, values, and goals, he'll prove he's the right person for the job."

***

When he returned home that night, Dave dropped his briefcase in his study and wandered into the kitchen carrying a brown paper bag and wearing a big smile.

Relaxing at the table, Dee looked up from the paper she was reading. "Hello, honey," she said as Dave gave her a peck on the cheek. "I hope you don't mind, but I'm having a pizza delivered tonight. I'm in the mood for something cheesy."

"Then tonight," Dave announced, "our humble pizza will be accompanied by Dom Pérignon." Dave pulled a bottle of cold champagne out of the bag.

"Oh, my! What's the occasion?" asked Dee as she went to the cupboard and got out two champagne flutes.

"We have three things to celebrate," said Dave. "One moment." He popped the bottle open and poured the champagne into the two glasses.

Raising his glass and putting on his best English accent, Dave said, "Lords, ladies, and gentlemen! May I crave your indulgence? It behooves me to proclaim—"

Dee giggled at Dave's imitation of the pompous wedding speech her father had prepared so diligently, mistakenly thinking it would fit the occasion. The "lords, ladies, and gentlemen" line had come to signal an important event a family member wanted to share without taking themselves too seriously.

"First of all, to you, my beloved wife, whose improving health fills my heart with joy. Thank you for crossing my path and choosing me so many years ago. Lord knows I don't deserve you."

Dee smiled as they clinked their glasses together. "Watch out," she joked, "if things get any cheesier we won't need the pizza!"

"Second, to Beattie Anderson, your brilliant sister and my early morning coffee buddy. Physically she may be halfway around the world, but she is with us in spirit. Not only was she here exactly when we needed her for love and support through your cancer scare, she also had a tremendous positive impact on my career by teaching me all about collaboration. More on that soon. For now, let's raise our glasses in absentia to the best bundle of beauty and brains in all of Britain."

"Hear, hear!" Dee chimed in. They clinked their glasses once again.

"Last and certainly least," Dave continued, "I humbly request that we raise a glass to *moi,* who—through a bit of hard work and a willingness to be coached by said sister-in-law—has today been named chief operating officer of Cobalt Enterprises!"

Dee shrieked with delight, throwing her arms around Dave as he leaned in for a kiss.

"How exciting for you, darling! And Beattie will be so proud that she played a part in it. Every cloud really does have a silver lining." Just then, the front doorbell announced the welcome arrival of the pizza delivery person.

As the couple sat in their kitchen, washing down their pizza with Dom Pérignon, Dave thought about how gloomy his outlook had been just a little over six months ago—and how surprisingly bright the future had suddenly become.

Epilogue

Dave slipped unseen into the back of the meeting room. The few dozen people inside were seated around tables, noisily engaged in brainstorming. One person at each table was standing by a flip chart, capturing ideas being shouted out by the others at the table.

Wayne, who had been part of a lively conversation at one of the tables, spotted Dave and walked to the back to join him.

"Hey, buddy," Wayne said. "What's up?"

"I just wanted to check in with you before I head out on vacation," Dave said.

"Sure you can't stay?" asked Wayne. "We could use your input."

"What's the topic?"

"Generating ideas for Primo IV," said Wayne. "With the first Primo project, we pleased the client. With Primo II and III, we figured out how to please the client and make a profit. Now we're hoping to please the client, make a profit, *and* make the product environmentally sustainable. It's a sticky problem, but I'm intrigued by a lot of the ideas I've heard here today."

As he listened, Dave reflected on the visible transformation he had witnessed in Wayne this past year. Even though Wayne had stepped up to a greater leadership role as head of the

Primo line, his ego had stepped down. A year ago Wayne never would have said he was intrigued by anyone's ideas but his own.

Teaching Cobalt's entire workforce about the Heart, the Head, and the Hands of collaboration had changed a lot of people. The UNITE acronym was alive and well. Dave was seeing even more diversity in recruits and new hires who were bringing in new and different ways of thinking. More important, because feedback sessions had been hardwired into operations, people felt safe to come forward with new ideas. The company's purpose, values, and goals, now brought up on a regular basis, had a clear impact on employees' behavior and decision making. Enhanced by new technologies, communication now flowed up, down, across, inside, and outside the organization. People at every level felt empowered to contribute in a variety of ways, including brainstorming sessions such as this one.

"I hope you're vacationing someplace special," said Wayne. "How long will you be gone?"

"Three weeks. And yes, it's a special place, particularly for Dee."

"That's great," said Wayne. "Where are you taking her? Bali? Cancun? Fiji?"

Dave shook his head. "Think Big Ben, Westminster Abbey, Buckingham Palace—"

Wayne frowned. "You're spending three weeks in London at this time of year? Why not someplace warm?"

"Because there's nothing warmer than family—and Dee and I have someone very special to visit." Dave headed for the door. "Good luck with Primo IV, Wayne. I know it's in good hands."

PART II

Tools and Resources to Create Collaboration

Self Assessment

How Collaborative Do You Think You Are?

The following assessment offers an opportunity for you to look at yourself as a collaborative leader or individual contributor. By examining questions pertaining to the five categories of Dave's UNITE model within the Heart, Head, and Hands domains of collaboration, you can see where your strengths are and where you need more work.

After taking the assessment yourself, give it to your peers, managers, and direct reports and ask them to fill it out as they think about you. It can be an eye opener to find out that your perspective on yourself is sometimes different from how others see you. With minor changes, this assessment can also be used to measure levels of collaboration within work groups, departments, and organizations.

Directions

Circle the letter that best represents you for each statement:

H = Hardly ever; **S** = Sometimes; **O** = Often; **V** = Very often; **A** = Always

After you complete the assessment, follow the directions on page 140 to find out how you scored.

THE HEART DOMAIN

Who You Are as a Collaborator: Your Character and Intentions

U—Utilize Differences

I believe everyone has something to contribute.	H S O V A
I ensure everyone is heard.	H S O V A
I actively seek different points of view.	H S O V A
I encourage debate about ideas.	H S O V A
I am comfortable with facilitating conflict.	H S O V A

N—Nurture Safety and Trust

I encourage people to speak their mind.	H S O V A

I consider all ideas before decisions are made.　H S O V A

I share knowledge freely.　H S O V A

I view mistakes as learning opportunities.　H S O V A

I am clear with others about what I expect.　H S O V A

THE HEAD DOMAIN

What You Know: Beliefs and Attitudes About Collaboration

I—Involve Others in Crafting a Clear Purpose, Values, and Goals

My team is committed to a shared purpose.　H S O V A

I know the purpose of our project and why it is important.　H S O V A

I hold myself and others accountable for adhering to our values.　H S O V A

I check decisions against our stated values.　H S O V A

I hold myself and others accountable for project outcomes.　H S O V A

THE HANDS DOMAIN

What You Do: Your Actions and Behavior During Collaboration

T—Talk Openly

I am considered a good listener. H S O V A

I share information about myself H S O V A
with my teammates.

I seek information and ask   H S O V A
questions.

I give constructive feedback and H S O V A
am open to feedback from oth-
ers.

I encourage people to network   H S O V A
with others.

E—Empower Yourself and Others

I continually work to develop my H S O V A
competence.

I feel empowered to give my   H S O V A
opinion during idea sessions,
even if I disagree.

I actively build and share my   H S O V A
network with others.

I share my skills and knowledge H S O V A
with other departments.

I believe my work is important   H S O V A
to the organization.

Scoring Instructions

1.   Enter the number of H S O V A responses under each letter of UNITE.
2.   Multiply your **H** responses by 1, **S** by 2, **O** by 3, **V** by 4, and **A** by 5. Enter the results on the bottom line for each section.
3.   Add numbers on the bottom line of each section to determine your total score for that section; then add totals together for your final score.

U   H   S   O   V   A

—   —   —   —   —

multiply by

1   2   3   4   5

—   —   —   —   —   **Score U** ____

N   H   S   O   V   A

—   —   —   —   —

multiply by

1   2   3   4   5

—   —   —   —   —   **Score N** ____

I   H   S   O   V   A

—   —   —   —   —

multiply by

1   2   3   4   5

—   —   —   —   —   **Score I** ____

T   H   S   O   V   A

—   —   —   —   —

multiply by

1   2   3   4   5

—   —   —   —   —   **Score T** ____

E   H   S   O   V   A

—   —   —   —   —

multiply by

1   2   3   4   5

—   —   —   —   —   **Score E** ____

Scoring Legend

The legend below will give you an idea of how strong you are in each area of the UNITE model.

21–25: Outstanding. Keep up the good work.

17–20: Very good. You are definitely on the right track.

14–16: Average. Keep working at it.

< 13: Poor. Pay attention—there is lots of room for improvement.

Questions to Ponder

- In which area did I score the highest?
- In which area did I score the lowest? What actions can I take to improve my skills or attitudes in this area?
- Did the results surprise me? How?

Collaboration

Best Practices

Regardless of your role, *you* can make a difference in helping create a culture of collaboration within your organization. The following section demonstrates attitudes you can adopt and actions you can take to build a collaborative environment, whether you are a leader or an individual contributor. Pay particular attention to the areas in which you scored in the average or poor ranges on the self assessment.

The HEART Domain of Collaboration

Utilize Differences

- **Be a role model.**
  - _ Acknowledge to yourself and others that you don't have all the answers.
  - _ Embrace new approaches; seek and value unique perspectives.
- **Actively seek opinions from a variety of sources.**
  - _ Reach out for input from other departments and functions.
  - _ Engage a variety of people in discussions.
  - _ Encourage introverts who may be uncomfortable speaking out.
  - _ Make sure every voice is heard, regardless of title or role.
  - _ Ask questions and praise candid answers.
  - _ Remember: diverse perspectives lead to innovation and decisions for the greater good.
- **Promote the idea that polite disagreement is constructive.**
  - _ Encourage respectful debate around issues; support differing viewpoints.

_ Take a facilitator role if difficulties arise; seek to understand concerns behind each stated position.

_ Get training and train others in giving/receiving feedback and in conflict resolution.

_ Airing of different perspectives can ultimately build trusting relationships.

The HEART Domain of Collaboration

Nurture Safety and Trust

- **Be a role model.**

  _ Share knowledge freely to model what you expect of others.

  _ Encourage others to speak freely without fear of judgment.

  _ Welcome all ideas and consider them before decisions are made.

  _ Give and receive feedback as a gift, without judgment or defensiveness.

  _ Be accessible, authentic, and dependable.

- **Build trust.**

  _ View mistakes and failures as learning opportunities; discuss openly.

  _ Encourage cross-functional and cross-generational mentoring at all levels.

_ Provide learning events that focus on trust building and team development.

- **Cultivate a safe, collaborative environment.**

  _ Be transparent when making decisions.

  _ Be sure people know their role and what a good job looks like.

  _ Share responsibility and power among all levels.

  _ Develop common goals and strategies and clear areas of responsibility.

  _ Give people freedom and space to experiment and innovate.

The HEAD Domain of Collaboration

Involve Others in Crafting a Clear Purpose, Values, and Goals

- **Be a role model.**
  _ A clear, shared purpose galvanizes action; values guide behavior; and goals focus energy.
  _ The project leader must ensure vision and direction are clear.
  _ Get feedback from everyone when crafting the purpose statement, operating values, and strategic goals for the project.
  _ Demonstrate a commitment to the greater good.
  _ Focus on continual improvement and, ultimately, organizational success.
  _ Have accountability standards for yourself and others.
  _ Show your colleagues what values look like as behaviors.
- **Align your project's purpose and values to those of the organization.**
  _ Assure that the goals and strategies put into practice drive your purpose.
  _ Rank values in order of importance.
  _ Check every decision you and the project team make against stated values.

_ Project team should define what collaboration means for this project: use collaborative language and commit to collaborative practices.

The HEAD Domain of Collaboration

- **Create a charter for every project.**
  _ Make sure everyone is clear on purpose, goals, roles, and the metrics for which they will be held accountable.
  _ In times of difficulty, refer to the charter agreements for guidance.
  _ Together with the project group, periodically review the charter to keep it top of mind and ensure it is relevant to the needs of the project.
  _ Use the charter as a vehicle for onboarding new people.

The HANDS Domain of Collaboration

Talk Openly

- **Be a role model.**
  _ Listen to understand.
  _ Share all relevant information.

_ Give constructive feedback and be open to feedback from others.

_ Encourage spontaneous interaction.

_ Seek information and ask questions.

_ Have an open door policy.

_ Encourage candor with respect.

- **Promote sharing and learning.**

_ Encourage networking among all departments and at all levels.

_ Create opportunities for cross functional teaming on projects.

_ Take time to evaluate meetings to maximize effective communication.

_ Train your people in communication skills and team development.

Empower Yourself and Others

- **Be a role model.**

_ Share your knowledge and experience.

_ Network with others across the organization.

_ Speak up in meetings.

_ Be a continual learner.

- **Empower each other.**

_ Encourage cross-functional reciprocation.

_ Build trust and reciprocity through sharing and networking.

_ Make sure you and your colleagues have competence and clarity on tasks and goals.

_ Involve other departments in idea generation sessions and decision making.

_ Create sharing opportunities such as brown bag lunches and workshops.

Acknowledgments

The authors are grateful for the unique bond created through this collaborative effort—the shared belief in the importance of workplace collaboration, the listening and learning, the laughter, and the respect shown for all points of view.

They thank Steve Piersanti for his provocative challenges and expert advice that sharpened the book's focus, message, and application; Martha Lawrence for her infectious enthusiasm and expert revisions to the early drafts; Renee Broadwell for her skilled editing, gentle diplomacy, and upbeat attitude; and everyone who reviewed the book and provided valuable feedback.

Thanks also go to colleague and friend Don Carew, senior consulting partner with The Ken Blanchard Companies, for being a great support as well as a model of the Heart, Head, and Hands—a true collaborator.

Finally, a One Minute Praising to Michael Murphy and the staff at Sharp Memorial Hospital in San Diego: throughout the course of Ken's two hip replacement surgeries, he witnessed a culture of exceptional collaboration and service, which helped inspire the world class hospital environment described in this story.

About the Authors

Ken Blanchard

Few people have made a more positive and lasting impact on the day-to-day management of people and companies than Ken Blanchard. He is the coauthor of several bestselling books, including the blockbuster international bestseller *The New One Minute Manager* ® and the giant business bestsellers *Raving Fans* and *Gung Ho!* His books have combined sales of more than twenty million copies in forty-two languages. Ken and his wife, Margie, are cofounders of The Ken Blanchard Companies®, a worldwide human resource development company. Ken is also cofounder of Lead Like Jesus, a nonprofit organization dedicated to inspiring and equipping people to be servant leaders in the marketplace. Ken and Margie live in San Diego and work with their son, Scott, his wife, Madeleine, and their daughter, Debbie.

Jane Ripley, B.Ed., MSc.

Jane's work life has been shaped by three significant experiences having to do with leadership and collaboration: watching her father struggle in his career, serving in the British army, and working with The Ken Blanchard Companies.

As a teenager, Jane watched her father, Bill, struggle as a union worker in the hostile environment of the UK motor industry of the 1970s. Strike after long strike defined her father's pattern of work. Bill always felt that collaboration would be a better way forward and was frustrated that neither side could see they needed each other.

In the 1980s, Jane joined the British army as an officer in the Women's Royal Army Corps (WRAC). During her six-year tenure, she found important agreement among the ranks: the army understood the value of collaboration. In fact, after leaving the army, Jane did not experience this higher level of collaboration again until she joined The Ken Blanchard Companies in 2006.

In 2012, Jane chose the topic of collaboration for her dissertation toward an M.S. in business psychology. Her research led to the writing of this book.

Jane is cofounder of Wired Leaders (www.wiredleaders.com), a leadership development company that focuses on collaboration.

Eunice Parisi-Carew, Ed.D.

Eunice's expertise lies in the areas of leadership, teams, and organizational change. With over thirty-five years of experience working with teams, she brings a practitioner's knowledge of the power of teams as a strategy, and a broad view of the culture that supports them.

Eunice is coauthor of three bestselling books: *The One Minute Manager Builds High Performing Teams, High Five,* and *Leading at a Higher Level.* She has written several articles and assessments regarding teams, women in leadership, and collaboration.

Eunice is co-creator of the High Performing Teams product line offered by The Ken Blanchard Companies, where she is a senior consultant. She is also cofounder of two independent small companies, In Her Own Voice and Wired Leaders. Eunice is on the board and a faculty member for the Masters of Science in

Executive Leadership program at the University of San Diego.

Eunice received her doctorate in the behavioral sciences from the University of Massachusetts, Amherst. She is a former board and faculty member of NTL Institute, a licensed psychologist, and a certified organizational consultant.

Services Available

The Ken Blanchard Companies ®

The Ken Blanchard Companies is committed to helping leaders and organizations perform at a higher level. The concepts and beliefs presented in this book are just a few of the ways that our global network of world class consultants, trainers, and coaches has helped organizations around the world improve workplace productivity, employee satisfaction, and customer loyalty. For more information, please contact us.

The Ken Blanchard Companies
World Headquarters
125 State Place
Escondido, California 92029
United States
+1-760-489-5005
International@kenblanchard.com
www.kenblanchard.com

The Ken Blanchard Companies UK
+44 (0) 1483 456300
UK@kenblanchard.com

The Ken Blanchard Companies Canada
+1 800 665 5023

Canada@kenblanchard.com

The Ken Blanchard Companies Singapore
+65-6775 1030
Singapore@kenblanchard.com

For an up-to-date list of all global partners of The Ken Blanchard Companies, including contact information, please go to www.kenblanchard.com/About-Us/Global-Locations.

Wired Leaders

Cofounded by Jane Ripley, Wired Leaders is a leadership development company that focuses on collaboration at every level and offers assessments, training, and consulting. For more information, please visit www.wiredleaders.com

Also by Ken Blanchard
Ken Blanchard and Mark Miller
Great Leaders Grow
Becoming a Leader for Life

What is the secret to lasting as a leader? As Ken Blanchard and Mark Miller write, "The path to increased influence, impact, and leadership effectiveness is paved with personal growth ... Our capacity to grow determines our capacity to lead." In *Great Leaders Grow,* Debbie Brewster becomes a mentor to Blake, her own mentor's young son. She tells him: "How well you and I serve will be determined by the decision to grow or not. Will you be a leader who is always ready to face the next challenge? Or will you be a leader who tries to apply yesterday's solutions to today's problems?" As Debbie leads Blake through the four growth areas that every leader must focus on, you'll be inspired to make your own long-term plan for professional and personal growth.

BK® Berrett–Koehler Publishers, Inc.
www.bkconnection.com

Ken Blanchard and Mark Miller
The Secret
**What Great Leaders Know and Do, Third
 Edition**

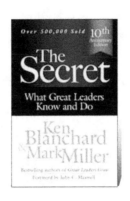

Join struggling young executive Debbie Brewster as she explores a profound yet seemingly contradictory concept: to lead is to serve. Along the way she learns why great leaders seem preoccupied with the future, what three arenas require continuous improvement, the two essential components of leadership success, how to knowingly strengthen—or unwittingly destroy—leadership credibility, and more.

Ken Blanchard and Jesse Lyn Stoner
Full Steam Ahead!
**Unleash the Power of Vision in Your Work
 and Your Life**

The lessons of *Full Steam Ahead!* are revealed through the inspirational story of two people who create an inspiring vision for the place they work and for their own lives. Together they discover the three elements of a compelling vision: a significant purpose, clear values, and a picture of the future. By understanding how a vision is created, communicated, and lived, they discover how to make that vision come alive.

Berrett–Koehler Publishers, Inc.
www.bkconnection.com

❀ Berrett–Koehler
BK̄ Publishers

Berrett-Koehler is an independent publisher dedicated to an ambitious mission: *connecting people and ideas to create a world that works for all.*

We believe that to truly create a better world, action is needed at all levels—individual, organizational, and societal. At the individual level, our publications help people align their lives with their values and with their aspirations for a better world. At the organizational level, our publications promote progressive leadership and management practices, socially responsible approaches to business, and humane and effective organizations. At the societal level, our publications advance social and economic justice, shared prosperity, sustainability, and new solutions to national and global issues.

A major theme of our publications is "Opening Up New Space." Berrett-Koehler titles challenge conventional thinking, introduce new ideas, and foster positive change. Their common quest is changing the underlying beliefs, mindsets, institutions, and structures that keep generating the same cycles of problems, no matter who our leaders are or what improvement programs we adopt.

We strive to practice what we preach—to operate our publishing company in line with the ideas in our books. At the core of our approach is stewardship, which we define as a deep sense of responsibility to administer the company for the benefit of all of our "stakeholder" groups: authors, customers, employees, investors, service providers, and the communities and environment around us.

We are grateful to the thousands of readers, authors, and other friends of the company who consider themselves to be part of the "BK Community." We hope that you, too, will join us in our mission.

A BK Business Book

This book is part of our BK Business series. BK Business titles pioneer new and progressive leadership and management practices in all types of public, private, and nonprofit organizations. They promote socially responsible approaches to business, innovative organizational change methods, and more humane and effective organizations.

Berrett–Koehler
Publishers

Connecting people and ideas
to create a world that works for all

Dear Reader,

Thank you for picking up this book and joining our worldwide community of Berrett-Koehler readers. We share ideas that bring positive change into people's lives, organizations, and society.

To welcome you, we'd like to offer you a free e-book. You can pick from among twelve of our bestselling books by entering the promotional code **BKP92E** here: http://www.bkconnection.com/welcome.www.bkconnection.com

When you claim your free e-book, we'll also send you a copy of our e-newsletter, the *BK Communiqué.* Although you're free to unsubscribe, there are many benefits to sticking around. In every issue of our newsletter you'll find

- A free e-book
- Tips from famous authors
- Discounts on spotlight titles
- Hilarious insider publishing news
- A chance to win a prize for answering a riddle

Best of all, our readers tell us, "Your newsletter is the only one I actually read." So claim your gift today, and please stay in touch!

Sincerely,

Charlotte Ashlock
Steward of the BK Website

Questions? Comments? Contact me at bkcomm unity@bkpub.com.

Certified

B Corporation

bcorporation.net

CPSIA information can be obtained
at www.ICGtesting.com
Printed in the USA
BVHW011318111220
595495BV00011B/55